DK Guide to DINOSAURS

David Lambert

DK

A Dorling Kindersley Book

LONDON, NEW YORK, MUNICH,
MELBOURNE, and DELHI

This book is dedicated to the scientists
whose research made it possible

Project Editor Ben Morgan
Project Art Editor Martin Wilson
Design Team Marcus James, Jane Tetzlaff,
Tory Gordon-Harris, Robin Hunter
Managing Editor Mary Ling
Managing Art Editor Rachael Foster
DTP Designer Almudena Díaz
Picture Research Angela Anderson
Photographer Gary Ombler
Jacket Design Hedi Gutt
Jacket Editor Mariza O'Keeffe
Production Kate Oliver
US Editor Gary Werner
Consultants Steve Hutt, Curator of the Museum of Isle of
Wight Geology; Dr A.C. Milner, Head of Fossil Vertebrates,
Natural History Museum, London
Paleontological Artist Luis Rey
Dinosaur Models Roby Braun, Jonathan Hately,
Graham High, Dennis Wilson & Gary Staab/Staab Studios
Computer Graphics Firelight Productions, Frank DeNota

Published in the United States by DK Publishing, Inc.
375 Hudson Street, New York, New York 10014

First American Edition, 2000
2 4 6 8 10 9 7 5 3

Copyright © 2000 Dorling Kindersley Limited
First paperback edition 2006

Library of Congress Cataloging-in-Publication Data

Lambert, David.
    DK guide to dinosaurs / by David Lambert. -- 1st American ed.
        p.   cm.
    Includes index
    Summary: Depicts how dinosaurs lived and died, covering such
topics as habitats, size, hunting techniques, self-defense, courtship,
and family life.
        ISBN-13: 978-0-7894-5237-5 ISBN-10: 0-7894-5237-5 (hardcover)
        ISBN-13: 978-0-7566-1793-6 ISBN-10: 0-7566-1793-6 (pbk.)
        1. Dinosaurs Juvenile literature. [1. Dinosaurs] I. Title
QE862.D5H93 2000
567.9--dc21   99-39207
                                                           CIP

Reproduced by Colourscan, Singapore
Printed and bound in China by Toppan Printing Co., Ltd.

Discover more at
www.dk.com

CONTENTS

WHAT IS A DINOSAUR?

DINOSAURS WERE AMONG the most amazing and successful animals ever. From ancestors no bigger than dogs, they evolved into gigantic killers as heavy as elephants, plant-eaters several bus-lengths long, and nimble little creatures the size of chickens. While they ruled the land, no mammal larger than a domestic cat survived. Dinosaurs first appeared about 230 million years ago and flourished for an astonishing 165 million years. Then, 65 million years ago, they suddenly and mysteriously disappeared. By comparison, modern humans have inhabited the Earth for only about 100,000 years.

RICHARD OWEN

DISCOVERING DINOSAURS

People have been finding dinosaur fossils for thousands of years, but the first to be identified as a giant extinct reptile was the fanged jawbone of *Megalosaurus* ("great lizard"), named in 1824 by William Buckland, a British naturalist. The term dinosaur ("terrible lizard") was coined by the British scientist Richard Owen in 1842.

MEGALOSAURUS JAW

Most dinosaurs had bare, scaly skin covered with tiny bumps.

KEY FEATURES

The dinosaurs were a group of mainly large, land-living reptiles. Like reptiles today, most had scaly skin (although some had feathers), a long tail, teeth, and claws on the fingers and toes. But while modern reptiles walk with their legs splayed sideways, dinosaurs walked upright with their legs directly below them, as mammals do. This key feature made many swift and agile on land.

Large tail for balance

Dinosaurs had an upright stance, with straight legs directly below their bodies.

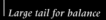

Lizards have a sprawling stance. Their legs are held sideways, and their elbows and knees bend at right angles.

Crocodiles have a semi-sprawling stance, with their knees and elbows slightly bent.

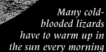

Many cold-blooded lizards have to warm up in the sun every morning in order to become active.

Muscular hindlegs

Birdlike feet

Some dinosaurs had a backward-pointing toe a little like the reversed toe of a bird's foot.

KEEP THE HEAT

Birds and mammals are warm-blooded, which means their body temperature is always the same. In contrast, reptiles are cold-blooded – they heat up and become active only when it is warm, and they cool down and become sluggish when it is cold. Were the dinosaurs warm- or cold-blooded? Most scientists think at least some flesh-eating dinosaurs were warm-blooded and that all big dinosaurs stayed warm because their bodies were too big to cool down at night.

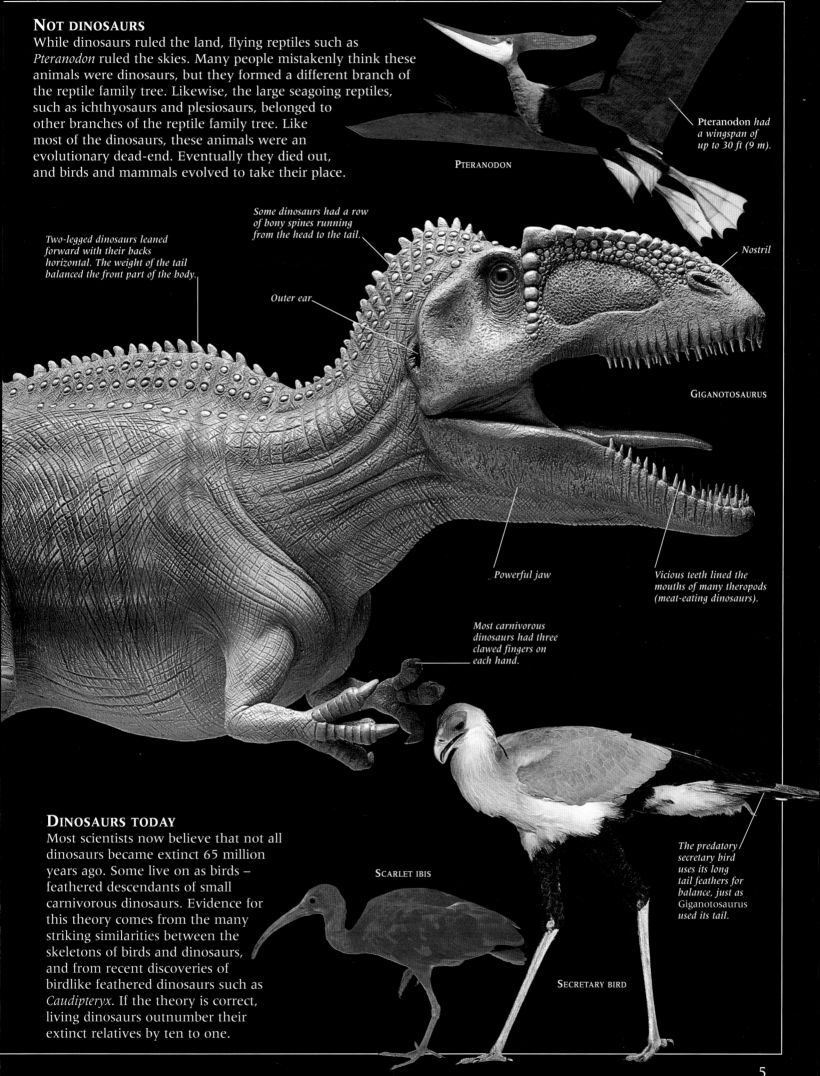

NOT DINOSAURS

While dinosaurs ruled the land, flying reptiles such as *Pteranodon* ruled the skies. Many people mistakenly think these animals were dinosaurs, but they formed a different branch of the reptile family tree. Likewise, the large seagoing reptiles, such as ichthyosaurs and plesiosaurs, belonged to other branches of the reptile family tree. Like most of the dinosaurs, these animals were an evolutionary dead-end. Eventually they died out, and birds and mammals evolved to take their place.

Pteranodon had a wingspan of up to 30 ft (9 m).

PTERANODON

Two-legged dinosaurs leaned forward with their backs horizontal. The weight of the tail balanced the front part of the body.

Some dinosaurs had a row of bony spines running from the head to the tail.

Nostril

Outer ear

GIGANOTOSAURUS

Powerful jaw

Vicious teeth lined the mouths of many theropods (meat-eating dinosaurs).

Most carnivorous dinosaurs had three clawed fingers on each hand.

DINOSAURS TODAY

Most scientists now believe that not all dinosaurs became extinct 65 million years ago. Some live on as birds – feathered descendants of small carnivorous dinosaurs. Evidence for this theory comes from the many striking similarities between the skeletons of birds and dinosaurs, and from recent discoveries of birdlike feathered dinosaurs such as *Caudipteryx*. If the theory is correct, living dinosaurs outnumber their extinct relatives by ten to one.

SCARLET IBIS

The predatory secretary bird uses its long tail feathers for balance, just as Giganotosaurus used its tail.

SECRETARY BIRD

PREHISTORIC EARTH

Duⁱng the age of dinosaurs – the Mesozoic Era – Planet Earth was very different from today. The climate was hotter, and the land was covered by deserts or strange prehistoric vegetation. The plants that dominate the land today – flowering plants – did not exist. Instead of grasses, there were ferns. Instead of broadleaved trees, there were forests of conifers, palmlike cycads, and tall tree ferns. The coastlines were unrecognizable. At the start of the Mesozoic, the continents were all joined together. Over millions of years, they broke up and drifted apart, carried by currents in the semi-molten rock deep below the planet's crust.

EARTH TODAY
This satellite image of Earth shows the planet's continents as they are now. The continents are still moving around, just as they were during the Mesozoic, although the movement is too slow for us to notice during a human lifetime. Millions of years from now, the Earth will be unrecognizable again.

EARTH TIMELINE
The Mesozoic stretched from 248 to 65 million years ago – an unimaginably long period of time, yet only a small fraction of the Earth's history. Scientists divide it into three distinct periods: the Triassic, the Jurassic, and the Cretaceous.

4,600 million years ago (mya)

TRIASSIC LIFE
Conifer

The first dinosaurs appeared in the Triassic Period, about 230 million years ago. They coexisted with crocodilians, lizards, pterosaurs (flying reptiles), and tortoises. Ferns and palmlike cycadeoids and cycads grew near streams, conifers on drier lands. But vast, hot deserts covered inland areas.

Horsetail plants
Cycad

JURASSIC LIFE
As continents fragmented, moist sea air shed rain on inland deserts. Here, cycads, cycadeoids, ferns, and horsetails grew near water, conifers on drier ground. Immense plant-eating and predatory dinosaurs eventually shared the land with the first birds and mammals, and with crocodilians and pterosaurs.

Cycad

CRETACEOUS LIFE
There were now more kinds of dinosaur than ever. Sharp-toothed plant-eaters grazed the flowering plants that were replacing older kinds of vegetation. Conifers and broadleaved trees that looked like today's appeared, as well as modern-looking frogs, snakes, birds, and mammals. But prehistoric reptiles still ruled the land, sea, and air.

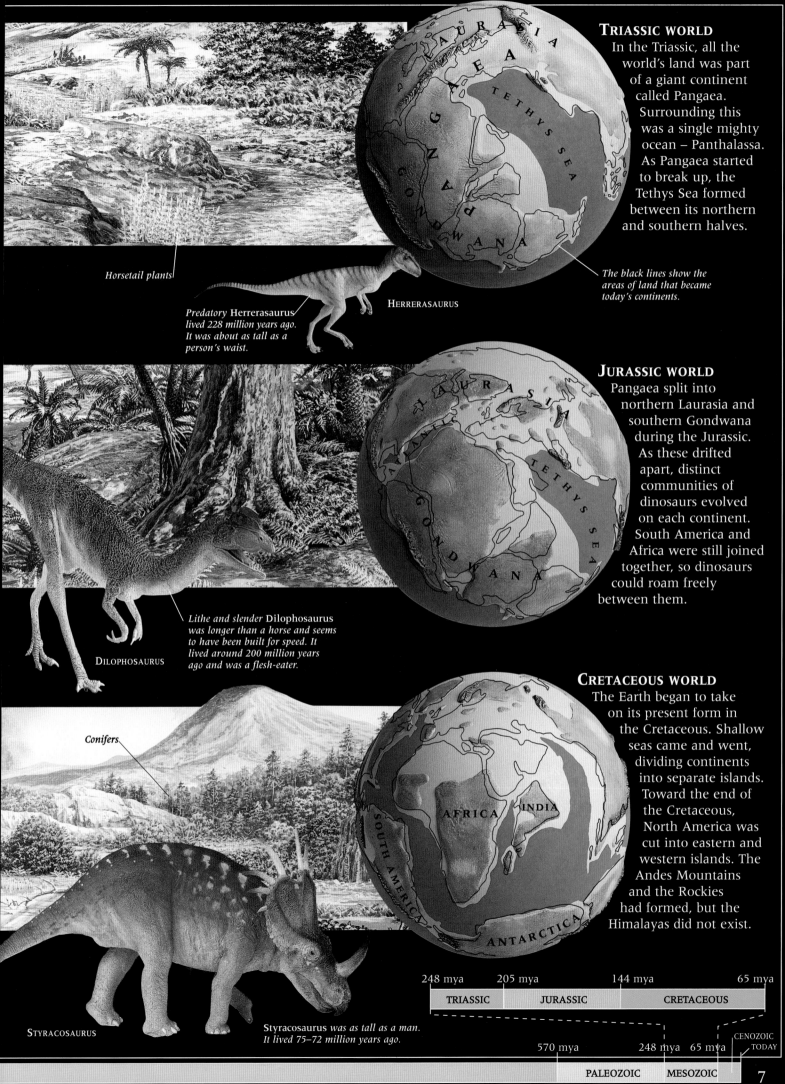

TRIASSIC WORLD

In the Triassic, all the world's land was part of a giant continent called Pangaea. Surrounding this was a single mighty ocean – Panthalassa. As Pangaea started to break up, the Tethys Sea formed between its northern and southern halves.

The black lines show the areas of land that became today's continents.

Horsetail plants

Predatory Herrerasaurus lived 228 million years ago. It was about as tall as a person's waist.

HERRERASAURUS

JURASSIC WORLD

Pangaea split into northern Laurasia and southern Gondwana during the Jurassic. As these drifted apart, distinct communities of dinosaurs evolved on each continent. South America and Africa were still joined together, so dinosaurs could roam freely between them.

Lithe and slender Dilophosaurus was longer than a horse and seems to have been built for speed. It lived around 200 million years ago and was a flesh-eater.

DILOPHOSAURUS

CRETACEOUS WORLD

The Earth began to take on its present form in the Cretaceous. Shallow seas came and went, dividing continents into separate islands. Toward the end of the Cretaceous, North America was cut into eastern and western islands. The Andes Mountains and the Rockies had formed, but the Himalayas did not exist.

Conifers

Styracosaurus was as tall as a man. It lived 75–72 million years ago.

STYRACOSAURUS

248 mya	205 mya	144 mya	65 mya
TRIASSIC	JURASSIC	CRETACEOUS	

570 mya	248 mya	65 mya	CENOZOIC TODAY
PALEOZOIC	MESOZOIC		

7

SIZE AND SCALE

THE WORD DINOSAUR makes us think of gigantic animals, yet dinosaurs came in a surprisingly wide range of sizes. The average dinosaur was probably no heavier than a horse, and many were far smaller. It may even be that fewer kinds of dinosaur weighed over a ton than did prehistoric land mammals (before human hunters began killing big mammals off). But as the fossil record proves, many dinosaurs were colossal. The biggest of them all – the long-necked sauropods – were the heaviest, longest, and tallest land animals ever. Only great whales weigh more than the heaviest dinosaur did.

THE MYTHICAL GIANT

This colossal leg is a reconstruction made by fossil-hunter Jim Jensen, who found fragments of a gigantic dinosaur in Colorado in the 1970s. Jensen believed he had discovered the heaviest dinosaur and called it "Ultrasaurus." But it turned out that the fragments came from different dinosaurs – the shoulder blade was from *Brachiosaurus*, and a piece of backbone was from a dinosaur called *Supersaurus*. The mix-up shows how difficult it can be even for experts to interpret fossil evidence.

BIGGEST KILLER

When scientists described it in 1995, *Giganotosaurus* from Argentina edged North America's *Tyrannosaurus* off its perch as the largest known flesh-eating dinosaur. *Giganotosaurus* was up to 41 ft (12.5 m) long and weighed 8 tons, compared with the 39 ft (12 m) and 6 tons of *Tyrannosaurus*, itself as heavy as an African bull elephant.

MIDGET CARNIVORE

If you met *Compsognathus* you might be astonished by how small dinosaurs could be. Fully grown, it was only the size of a turkey. About 150 million years ago, this diminutive predator prowled desert islands, seizing lizards and small mammals with its grasping fingers and tearing them apart with its sharp teeth or swallowing them whole. Smaller even than *Compsognathus*, though, was 20 in (50 cm) long plant-eating *Micropachycephalosaurus*, the shortest dinosaur with the longest name.

BIG-HEADED DINOSAUR

The horned dinosaur *Pentaceratops* might have had the largest head of any dinosaur (a claim that has been made for *Torosaurus*, too). Its big skull grew nearly 10 ft (3 m) long, although much of this was in the backswept bony frill. Rival males probably brandished frills by lowering their heads, and may have jousted at each other with their horns.

GIGANOTOSAURUS

COMPSOGNATHUS

BIGGEST OF ALL TIME

If *Barosaurus* strolled down a city street it would seem mind-blowingly huge. Yet there were sauropods even longer and heavier than this 75 ft (23 m) long colossus. At 40 tons in weight, *Brachiosaurus* was as heavy as 7 elephants; 70-ton *Supersaurus* weighed as much as 12 elephants or 1,000 people. Bigger still was *Seismosaurus,* the "earthquake lizard." At 164 ft (50 m) long, it could have spanned two tennis courts laid end to end; estimates of its weight range from 50 to 150 tons. Tantalizing finds of incomplete skeletons suggest that some sauropods grew even bigger than this. Perhaps one of these mysterious creatures – either *Argentinosaurus* or *Amphicoelias* – deserves the title "biggest-ever dinosaur."

BAROSAURUS

BEE HUMMINGBIRD

SMALLEST DINOSAUR

If paleontologists are right to classify birds as dinosaurs, then the tiniest dinosaur is the bee hummingbird of Cuba, which is barely larger than a bumblebee. This dinosaur is an expert at hovering in midair. Like a bumblebee, it collects nectar from flowers. Males weigh only 0.06 oz (1.6 g) and grow no longer from head to tail than a little finger.

GETTING AROUND

PEOPLE ONCE THOUGHT THAT MANY DINOSAURS were too heavy to live out of water and had to wallow in lakes, their long necks serving as snorkels. But careful studies have shown that all dinosaurs lived and walked on land. The biggest were four-legged with heavy club feet, so they probably moved slowly like elephants. Smaller two-legged dinosaurs were swifter and more nimble. The long-legged ornithomimids ("ostrich mimics") were probably the quickest, capable of sprinting at sustained high speeds.

ROAD RUNNERS

Perhaps no dinosaur outsprinted *Gallimimus* ("chicken mimic"), the largest ornithomimid. This tall, athletic animal might have run at 50 mph (80 kmh) – faster that the fastest racehorse. *Gallimimus* usually paced around slowly, snapping up seeds, insects, or small mammals, but it was always ready to dash off quickly if a predator appeared.

RUN LIKE AN OSTRICH

Gallimimus probably ran like an ostrich, using its powerful hindlegs to pound the ground in long strides. Unlike an ostrich, though, it had a long tail that acted as a rudder, keeping it balanced if it had to make sudden turns to outwit a predator.

Large round eye with bony eye-ring

Toothless beak

GALLIMIMUS SKULL

Gallimimus's skull resembled a bird's, with a long, flat, toothless beak and wide eye sockets. A ring of little bony plates protected each eye (a feature still seen in birds). The eyes faced sideways, enabling *Gallimimus* to spot enemies approaching from almost any direction. The braincase held a brain about the size of a golf ball (a little larger than an ostrich's).

LIVING IN HERDS

Apart from fossil footprints, there is little direct evidence that dinosaurs lived in herds. But so many animals today live in groups – from schools of fish to prides of lions – that paleontologists (fossil experts) think some dinosaurs probably did so, too. With more eyes and ears on the alert, it is easier for a herd to spot predators and find food. *Gallimimus* lived in a desert and may have had to travel long distances in search of food or water. Perhaps herds of *Gallimimus* made seasonal migrations like the animals of Africa's savannas.

The long tail was a counterbalance to the front of Gallimimus's body, allowing it to lean forward as it sprinted.

BUILT FOR SPEED

Scientists can tell this dinosaur was built for speed by comparing its anatomy with living animals. The chief clues are its lightly built body and long legs and feet. *Gallimimus* had shins longer than its thighs, a hallmark of fast sprinters like gazelles. Inside, it probably had a heart, lungs, and digestive organs like a bird's. We can guess this because birds are the closest living relatives of *Gallimimus*.

S-shaped neck

Stomach

Lungs

Heart

Muscular tail

Intestines

Cloaca

Thigh bone

Shin

Rib

Ankle

Foot

Toe

FOSSIL FINDS

GALLIMIMUS

TRIASSIC	JURASSIC	CRETACEOUS

248 205   144   65
Million years ago

FEET AND FOOTPRINTS

Dinosaurs' feet and legs were tremendously varied. Most of the large, four-legged plant-eaters had sturdy limbs and broad feet like an elephant's. Two-legged dinosaurs had long, birdlike feet and three toes, tipped with sharp claws or hooflike nails. Four-legged dinosaurs usually plodded along, but some two-legged dinosaurs were as fast as a horse. Scientists can tell how quickly a dinosaur moved by comparing it with mammals or birds of today with similar bone structure, or by studying dinosaur footprints. Tracks left in mud that later turned to rock offer valuable clues about the speed and motion of these animals.

Thigh bone

Knee

Shin bone

Ankle joint

Toe

TYRANNOSAURUS

Claw

Shin bone

Ankle joint

Big theropods like **Tyrannosaurus** *made big, birdlike footprints.*

Hadrosaurs made large, rounded three-toed footprints.

Sauropods made huge back-foot prints and smaller front-foot prints.

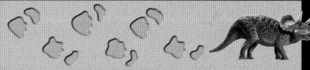

Ceratopsians made smaller double prints than those of sauropods.

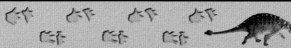

Armored dinosaurs made double prints with clear toe marks.

MAKING TRACKS

Dinosaur footprints have been found all over the world. Unfortunately, it is often difficult to tell which dinosaurs made them; but we can make an educated guess by comparing their shape with fossil foot bones. In some places there are parallel rows of prints, showing where a herd walked side by side. Some tracks even show footprints of flesh-eating dinosaurs overlapping plant-eaters' prints – perhaps evidence of a hunt.

TYRANNOSAURUS

Imagine a chicken leg grotesquely magnified and you get some idea of *Tyrannosaurus's* hindleg. Like modern birds, flesh-eating dinosaurs had long-shinned, scaly legs, each with three long, forward-pointing, claw-tipped toes. Another toe did not touch the ground but was set off to one side; in birds the same toe faces backward. *Tyrannosaurus's* legs were incredibly sturdy. The huge, pillarlike leg bones had to carry the weight of a 6-ton body.

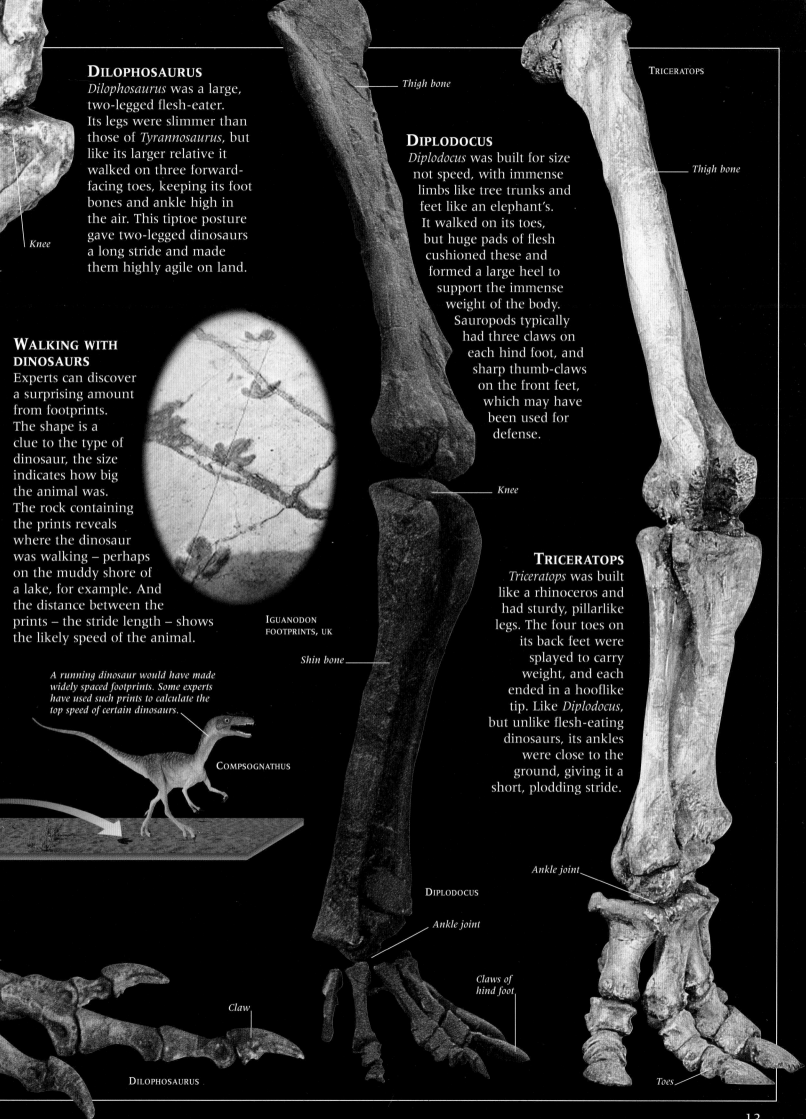

DILOPHOSAURUS

Dilophosaurus was a large, two-legged flesh-eater. Its legs were slimmer than those of *Tyrannosaurus*, but like its larger relative it walked on three forward-facing toes, keeping its foot bones and ankle high in the air. This tiptoe posture gave two-legged dinosaurs a long stride and made them highly agile on land.

Knee

WALKING WITH DINOSAURS

Experts can discover a surprising amount from footprints. The shape is a clue to the type of dinosaur, the size indicates how big the animal was. The rock containing the prints reveals where the dinosaur was walking – perhaps on the muddy shore of a lake, for example. And the distance between the prints – the stride length – shows the likely speed of the animal.

IGUANODON FOOTPRINTS, UK

A running dinosaur would have made widely spaced footprints. Some experts have used such prints to calculate the top speed of certain dinosaurs.

COMPSOGNATHUS

Claw

DILOPHOSAURUS

Thigh bone

DIPLODOCUS

Diplodocus was built for size not speed, with immense limbs like tree trunks and feet like an elephant's. It walked on its toes, but huge pads of flesh cushioned these and formed a large heel to support the immense weight of the body. Sauropods typically had three claws on each hind foot, and sharp thumb-claws on the front feet, which may have been used for defense.

Knee

Shin bone

DIPLODOCUS

Ankle joint

Claws of hind foot

TRICERATOPS

Thigh bone

TRICERATOPS

Triceratops was built like a rhinoceros and had sturdy, pillarlike legs. The four toes on its back feet were splayed to carry weight, and each ended in a hooflike tip. Like *Diplodocus*, but unlike flesh-eating dinosaurs, its ankles were close to the ground, giving it a short, plodding stride.

Ankle joint

Toes

UP IN THE AIR

ABOVE THE DINOSAURS flapped and soared strange, bat-like reptiles – the pterosaurs. Some were as small as sparrows, but others had the wingspan of a light aircraft. All had slim, hollow bones and wings made of skin that stretched between enormously long finger-bones and the legs. Like bats and birds today, pterosaurs may have been warm-blooded and furry. Most were fish-eaters that lived much like those seabirds the terns and frigate birds. There may also have been pterosaur "swallows" that caught insects in the air, and pterosaur "vultures" that ate carrion. The pterosaurs were relatives of the dinosaurs, but they were not dinosaurs themselves.

Dimorphodon's head and beak must have been lightweight, otherwise it would have toppled forward as it perched.

If pterosaurs were warm-blooded, they would have needed a layer of fur to conserve heat and keep them warm.

The short, spiky teeth of Dimorphodon suggest it probably preyed on fish.

Dimorphodon *folded its wings when it landed. The leading edge of each wing was formed by a finger bone that had become incredibly long.*

A flattened vane (rudder) at the end of the tail helped to control balance during flight.

The pterosaurs could probably gain height effortlessly by gliding in circles on thermals (updrafts of warm air).

DIMORPHODON

The pterosaur *Dimorphodon* looked like a cross between a puffin and a fruit bat. It had a large head and a deep, narrow snout like a puffin's beak, but lined with teeth. *Dimorphodon* grew to 1 m (3 ft 3 in) long, half of which consisted of a stiff tail that acted as a rudder. The wings were short for its overall size. Some experts have suggested that *Dimorphodon* ran on its long hindlegs, but new fossil finds show it walked on all fours and clawed its way up rocks or trees.

ON THE WING

Dimorphodon had wings made of skin that was stiffened by fibres. It used flight muscles much like a bird's to flap the wings. How fast it flew and how quickly it turned would have depended mainly on the size and width of its wings. It probably skimmed the sea, snatching up small fish between its sharp little teeth. If it came down on water, it could get airborne again by flapping its wings and kicking backward with its webbed feet.

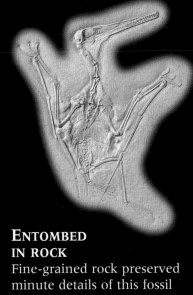

ENTOMBED IN ROCK

Fine-grained rock preserved minute details of this fossil pterosaur. An agile, narrow-winged flyer the size of a seagull, *Pterodactylus* swooped on small fish in late-Jurassic lagoons. It had teeth, like earlier pterosaurs, but no tail. As pterosaurs evolved, their teeth and tails got smaller to save weight and help them fly.

CRIORHYNCHUS

Wingspan up to 5 m (17 ft)

FANTASTIC FINGERS

With a wingspan the width of a badminton court, *Criorhynchus* zoomed over the sea like a gigantic albatross. A crest on the tip of its snout would have let its head slip easily out of the water as it snatched up a fish while still in the air. Huge, gliding pterosaurs such as *Criorhynchus* flourished in Cretaceous times in what is now England.

DIMORPHODON

CRIORHYNCHUS

TRIASSIC	JURASSIC	CRETACEOUS
248	205	144	65

Million years ago

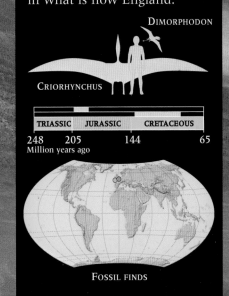

FOSSIL FINDS

15

BELOW THE WAVES

I F YOU WENT SCUBA DIVING during the Cretaceous Period, the underwater world would have looked much as it does today. The seas teemed with familiar animals – jellyfish, corals, oysters, crabs, snails, and a bewildering variety of fish, including sharks. But you might also have caught sight of some of the weird and wonderful reptiles that once lived in the oceans. Like dolphins and whales, the marine reptiles evolved from land animals that returned to the sea. These monsters of the deep dominated the oceans for more than 100 million years. Perhaps the strangest were the plesiosaurs – giant "sea serpents" that propelled themselves gracefully through the water with two pairs of flippers. Plesiosaurs died out in the mysterious mass extinction that also wiped out the dinosaurs, although a few people claim that they have survived in the form of the elusive Loch Ness monster.

Elasmosaurus had to rise to the surface of the water to breathe air, just like whales do today.

CRETOXYRHINA

One of the plesiosaurs' main enemies might have been a prehistoric shark called Cretoxyrhina, *which was as big as a great white shark.*

SNAKE NECKS

Plesiosaurs had paddlelike flippers, and many had small heads and long and extremely flexible necks. *Elasmosaurus* grew to about 46 ft (14 m) long; more than half of its total body length was taken up by the neck. Perhaps this extraordinary animal swam with its head held above the sea surface, plunging it down into the water now and again to snatch fish. Another possibility is that it rested on the bottom, occasionally darting its head up to grab passing fish.

Forward-facing, interlocking teeth

ELASMOSAURUS

TOOTHY TRAP

As *Cryptoclidus* shut its mouth, its long, slender teeth interlocked, trapping shrimps and small fish. Like all other plesiosaurs, this seagoing reptile had limbs that had evolved as flippers by adding extra toe and finger bones. Its 13 ft (4 m) long skeleton, found in Britain's late Jurassic rocks, was less than a third the length of *Elasmosaurus*. *Cryptoclidus* swallowed stones to reduce its natural buoyancy, allowing it to make deep dives in pursuit of its prey.

Each flipper was made up of five elongated fingers or toes.

CRYPTOCLIDUS

BREEDING

Elasmosaurus probably mated under water but it breathed air, so the female almost certainly laid eggs on land. Special enlarged ribs in the belly protected a female's soft internal tissues as her four flippers hauled her great body awkwardly ashore. She would have used her hind flippers to dig a hole in sand, where she laid and buried her eggs. Mothers, and later their hatchlings, risked dinosaur attacks as they flopped clumsily back to sea.

Elasmosaurus's *neck was so long that one scientist called it a "snake threaded through the body of a turtle".*

Plesiosaurs probably flapped their front and back flippers alternately like wings to "fly" through the water.

FOSSIL FINDS

ELASMOSAURUS

TRIASSIC	JURASSIC	CRETACEOUS
248	205	144	65

Million years ago

OCEAN CRUISERS

ICHTHYOSAURS ("FISH LIZARDS") WERE SEAGOING reptiles whose streamlined bodies made them ideal for chasing fast-swimming prey. Their large bodies tapered at both ends, and they braked, steered, and stayed upright with help from flippers, a dorsal fin, and an upright tail fin. Like plesiosaurs, ichthyosaurs had to breathe air at the surface and may have had lizardlike ancestors who once lived on land, but they would have been helpless ashore. The price they paid for speed in the water was being unable to leave it. Ichthyosaurs were born, grew up, and died in the sea.

Ichthyosaurus swam forward mainly by beating its tail from side to side, like a fish. In contrast, dolphins beat their tails up and down.

Ichthyosaurus's skin was smooth and thick.

Dorsal fin

Flipper

STENOPTERYGIUS

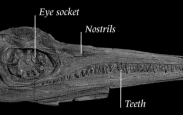

SHARK ATTACK

Like dolphins, the living sea mammals they so closely resembled, ichthyosaurs could have leapt clear of the water for fun. But it seems unlikely that these unintelligent reptiles would have been jumping for joy. If they leapt at all, it is most likely that they did so to escape from attacking sharks or to shake off parasites.

ICHTHYOSAURUS

An *Ichthyosaurus* and her young swim in a shallow sea where millions of years later western Europe would stand. Some ichthyosaur species grew five times longer than this 7 ft (2 m) creature, but none left more plentiful remains. After the first *Ichthyosaurus* was discovered in England, southern Germany's shale rocks yielded hundreds more skeletons of adults and young, making this one of the best known of all animals from the time of the dinosaurs.

The bones of the ear were huge to help pick up vibrations made by possible prey.

SEAFOOD DIET

Fast-moving squid, their prehistoric relatives belemnites and ammonites, and small fish were all snacks for the ichthyosaurs. Swift and agile, and capable of swimming at up to 25 mph (40 kmh), ichthyosaurs could outpace most prey. We know what ichthyosaurs ate from fish scales and belemnites' hooklets found in their stomachs and droppings.

SQUID

ICHTHYOSAURUS

Large eye for hunting by sight.

FOSSIL SKELETON

Superbly preserved ichthyosaur fossils like this *Stenopterygius* include the body's outline. This shows that some ichthyosaur fins had no bones to support them. For instance, the spine's downcurved end strengthened only the lower part of the tail. In some fossils even pigment cells survive. These hint that *Ichthyosaurus's* skin was dark reddish-brown.

Eye socket

Nostrils

Teeth

SKULL

Ichthyosaurus's skull had long, narrow jaws crammed with sharp teeth for gripping slippery victims. The creature surfaced to breathe through nostrils in front of its eyes. Big sockets show the eyes were large, for hunting in the sea's dimly lit upper layers. A ring of bony plates around each eye helped muscles alter the eye's shape to focus on prey.

ICHTHYOSAURUS

TRIASSIC	JURASSIC	CRETACEOUS	
248	205	144	65

Million years ago

BABY ICHTHYOSAURUS

As they were unable to lay eggs ashore, ichthyosaurs gave birth to their babies under water as whales do today. Scientists know this because partly formed babies were found inside some of the fossil ichthyosaurs that have been discovered. The skeletons of the babies were not broken up as they would have been if they had been swallowed and partly digested.

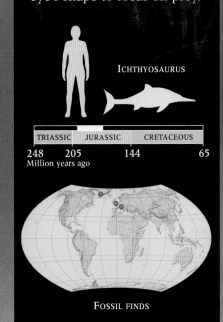

FOSSIL FINDS

MIGRATION

E VERY YEAR, MANY ANIMALS set off on long-distance journeys to find food or breeding sites. Their journeys are called migrations. In North America, caribou trek thousands of miles north every spring to feed in the Arctic. In autumn, they head south again to escape the bitter northern winter. Birds cover even greater distances – in a single year the Arctic tern can fly up to 12,000 miles (20,000 km). Dinosaurs may have migrated for much the same reason. Our strongest clues that they did so are fossil remains of certain dinosaurs that have been found in the north of Alaska as well as thousands of miles farther south.

The dotted red line shows the route migrating dinosaurs might have taken to reach the Arctic Circle. Earth's continents were becoming recognizable by this stage of the late Cretaceous.

Rockies

Migration route

AFRICA

SOUTH AMERICA

THE QUEST FOR THE POLE

The Arctic dinosaurs of North America may have migrated up the coastal plains that once lay between the Rocky Mountains and the western shore of a sea called the Niobrara Seaway. In late Cretaceous times this shallow sea ran from the Arctic Ocean to the Gulf of Mexico, splitting the continent into western and eastern islands. One of the migrants may have been the horned dinosaur *Pachyrhinosaurus*, whose fossils have been found in both Alberta, Canada, and the north coast of Alaska, 2,200 miles (3,500 km) away.

Migrating dinosaurs would probably have traveled in herds for protection from predators. Fossil remains indicate that Pachyrhinosaurus may have lived in herds tens of thousands strong.

STRANGE SKULL

Pachyrhinosaurus ("thick-nosed lizard") gets its name from a bony lump on the nose where other horned dinosaurs had a sharp horn. Rival males 21 ft (6.5 m) long might have faced each other and used these weird lumps, or "nasal bosses," in head-to-head shoving contests.

PACHYRHINOSAURUS

Nasal boss

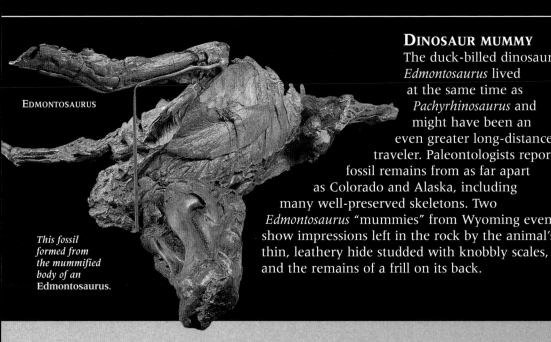

EDMONTOSAURUS

*This fossil
formed from
the mummified
body of an
Edmontosaurus.*

DINOSAUR MUMMY

The duck-billed dinosaur
Edmontosaurus lived
at the same time as
Pachyrhinosaurus and
might have been an
even greater long-distance
traveler. Paleontologists report
fossil remains from as far apart
as Colorado and Alaska, including
many well-preserved skeletons. Two
Edmontosaurus "mummies" from Wyoming even
show impressions left in the rock by the animal's
thin, leathery hide studded with knobbly scales,
and the remains of a frill on its back.

FOSSIL FINDS

PACHYRHINOSAURUS

TRIASSIC	JURASSIC	CRETACEOUS
248	205	144	65

Million years ago

EPIC TREK

Seventy million years ago, you might have seen herds of
Pachyrhinosaurus trudging north each spring from what is
now Alberta in Canada. These lumbering plant-eaters
would have been lured north by lush, large-leafed plants
in northern Alaska. There, only 10 degrees south of the
North Pole, the Sun did not set in summer and the
climate was much warmer than today. Walking an
estimated 31 miles (50 km) a day, a *Pachyrhinosaurus*
herd would have taken more than two months to
reach its destination. When the leaves withered and
fell in Alaska, they would set off on their return trek.

HAZARDOUS JOURNEYS

Migrating animals face grave hazards on their journeys. African
wildebeest risk attack by crocodiles as they cross rivers to reach
rain-fed pastures. Migrating dinosaurs would have faced similar
dangers, perhaps also falling victim to crocodilians. The tyrannosaur
Albertosaurus might have stalked *Pachyrhinosaurus* herds, picking off
the weak or young. In Alberta, thousands of *Pachyrhinosaurus* once
perished together, perhaps while fording a rain-swollen river.

JURASSIC GIRAFFES

THE SAUROPODS WERE THE TALLEST, longest, and heaviest animals ever to walk the Earth. Fully grown, some weighed as much as 15 African elephants. Size was their main form of self-defense – they were simply too big to attack. And this was not the only advantage of being a giant. Standing high off the ground, a sauropod could crop leafy twigs out of reach of all other plant-eating dinosaurs. Sauropods were strictly herbivorous. Like leaf-eaters today, they would have had to spend nearly all their time feeding just to stay alive.

Brachiosaurus *roamed open countryside where trees mainly grew near swamps and lakes that dried up during the hot summers.*

BAROSAURUS

Barosaurus had stocky limbs, a very long neck, and a long, slender tail. Like its better-known relative *Diplodocus*, it probably had a small skull and peg-shaped teeth for stripping leaves off plants. If it reared up on its hind legs it might have browsed on treetops four storys high. However, experts now suspect it was more of a "hedge cutter" than a high-level feeder.

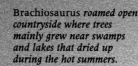

BAROSAURUS

Barosaurus used its long tail for balance as it moved.

Like most sauropods, Barosaurus probably could not raise its long neck high, although it could swing the neck sideways as it fed.

The rounded end of this Barosaurus *vertebra fitted into a hollow in the next vertebra.*

IMPOSSIBLE NECKS

Sauropods' necks look impossibly long until you know how they were made. Each neck contained a row of interlocking spinal bones, or vertebrae. These were reinforced below by thin, bony neck-ribs that overlapped each other and stiffened the neck. Above the vertebrae ran muscles, ligaments, and tendons that braced the neck and controlled its movements

BRACHIOSAURUS

Brachiosaurus resembled an immense giraffe, with nostrils in the bulge above its eyes. Its strong, chisel-shaped teeth could have chopped off woody twigs. Perhaps it browsed among the treetops. However, some scientists think its muscles could not raise the neck very steeply, and, even if they could, its heart would not have been strong enough to pump blood up to the brain.

Trees nibbled by sauropods would have lost all twigs and leaves up to a certain level. African acacias nibbled by giraffes show just such a browse line.

INSIDE SAUROPODS

The tough vegetation that sauropods ate had to be ground up to release its nutrients, but sauropods' simple teeth were no good for grinding. Bits of polished stone found in sauropod fossils suggest they had a gizzard – a churning muscular stomach containing a mill of swallowed stones that mashed food to a pulp. Many birds and reptiles today, including crocodiles, have a gizzard for this purpose.

Neck muscles

Vertebra

Small intestine

Lung

Heart

Gizzard

Cloaca

Large intestine

Elbow

Wrist

BRACHIOSAURUS

BRACHIOSAURUS

TRIASSIC	JURASSIC	CRETACEOUS

248   205   144   65
Million years ago

CRETACEOUS COWS

THE HADROSAURS WERE THE CRETACEOUS equivalent of cows. They lived toward the end of the Age of Dinosaurs, when they wandered in giant herds through the forests and swamps of North America, constantly munching on ferns, pine needles, leaves, and flowers. Instead of claws, they had hoofed fingertips that allowed them to wade in water or walk on soft ground on all fours. They probably spent most of their lives on open ground, where they could sprint on their hind legs to escape predators such as *Tyrannosaurus*.

The stiff tail probably could not swing from side to side.

CORYTHOSAURUS

CORYTHOSAURUS

Apart from its crest, Parasaurolophus *looked similar to* Corythosaurus.

PARASAUROLOPHUS

TROMBONE HEAD

The hadrosaur *Parasaurolophus* had an even stranger crest than *Hypacrosaurus*. Scientists have come up with all kinds of theories to explain its shape, suggesting, for example, that it might have been a snorkel for breathing underwater or an extension of its nose for extra-sensitive smelling. The current theory is that *Parasaurolophus* could blow through the crest to make honking noises like a trombone.

DEATH POSE

Corythosaurus was a typical member of the hadrosaur family. This *Corythosaurus* skeleton shows the exact position in which one of these dinosaurs was buried, lying on its side, by mud and sand about 70 million years ago. The well-preserved fossil shows a lattice of thin bones crisscrossing the backbones. These would have held the tail stiffly in the air when *Corythosaurus* was walking.

FOSSIL SKULL

Hadrosaurs had ducklike beaks for stripping vegetation, and tightly packed rows of teeth to grind their food. Many also had a distinctive crest on the head, as in this *Hypacrosaurus*. Scientists are not sure what the crest was for, but it seems to have been larger in males. Perhaps the males used their crests to attract females, just as deer use their antlers today.

Crest

Teeth

Ducklike beak

SWAMPLAND

Most hadrosaurs lived in warm plains between the Rocky Mountains and a vast inland sea that divided North America into western and eastern halves. As well as cypress swamps, there were pine forests, fern prairies, and coastal marshes. The first flowering plants – the plants and trees that dominate the world today – were just beginning to spread.

FOSSIL FINDS

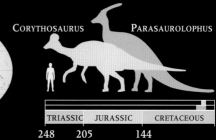

CORYTHOSAURUS   PARASAUROLOPHUS

TRIASSIC	JURASSIC	CRETACEOUS
248	205	144

Million years ago

HUNTING IN PACKS

NOT ALL DINOSAURS were docile plant-eaters. The flesh-eating dinosaurs – theropods – had to kill to survive. Lethal weapons equipped these animals for a life of violence: razor-sharp fangs, claws like grappling hooks, powerful jaws for tearing flesh, and muscular legs to stamp the life out of small victims. Many would have preyed on small fry – baby dinosaurs, lizards, or eggs. Others may have ganged together, using stealth and cunning to trap larger victims, and teamwork to overwhelm them. One of the most savage of these pack-hunters might have been the theropod *Velociraptor*.

SPEEDY KILLER

Velociraptor ("swift robber") was the two-legged dinosaurian equivalent of a lithe, agile hunting cat. This theropod was not as fast as a cheetah, and only about as bright as a bird, but it packed more killing power than almost any creature of its weight. Its weapons were long, narrow jaws bristling with bladelike fangs, and fingers and toes armed with sharply curved, daggerlike claws.

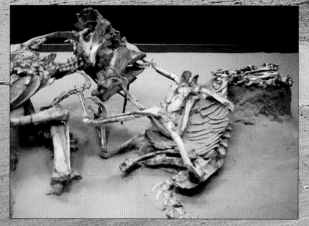

DUEL TO THE DEATH

Fossils of a *Velociraptor* and a *Protoceratops* that died locked in battle over 70 million years ago hint at their fighting techniques. The 7 ft (2 m) long *Velociraptor* had grappled with the pig-sized *Protoceratops*. The theropod tried grasping its victim's snout with clawed hands while kicking savagely at its throat. As it died, the *Protoceratops* clamped its strong "parrot's beak" on the aggressor's right arm. Before the *Velociraptor* broke free, windblown sand seems to have smothered them both.

VELOCIRAPTOR

Velociraptor's chief weapons were its sickle-shaped second-toe claws, which swung forward to deliver slashing attacks.

Velociraptor's long arms folded back against its body. When it leaped on its prey, the arms unfolded with a twist of the wrist, just as birds unfold their wings to fly. Stretching out, it then hooked its claws in a victim's hide.

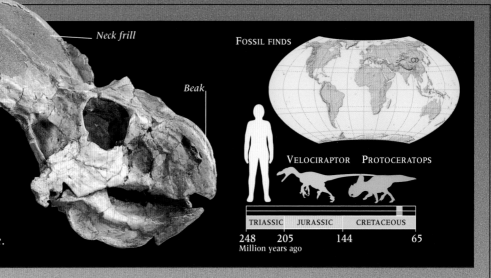

PROTOCERATOPS

Protoceratops ("first horned face") had a large bony neck frill but lacked the horns of larger, more advanced horned dinosaurs. This four-legged plant-eater probably cropped tough-leaved plants with its "parrot's beak" and sliced them up with sharp cheek teeth that cut like scissors. Weighed down by its head, it might not have run very fast. If attacked, biting would have been its most effective defense.

Neck frill

Beak

FOSSIL FINDS

VELOCIRAPTOR   PROTOCERATOPS

| TRIASSIC | JURASSIC | CRETACEOUS | |

248   205   144   65
Million years ago

A member of the pack lurks expectantly in the background, waiting to go in for the kill. Packs of Velociraptors *may have encircled their prey in the same way that lions do.*

PROTOCERATOPS

Perhaps Velociraptor *had a "scissor-hands" style of attack, flicking its wrists repeatedly until the victim was slashed to ribbons.*

ARMS AND CLAWS

DINOSAURS TENDED TO HAVE shorter arms than legs because they evolved from two-legged running ancestors that used their arms just for grabbing prey. Most predatory dinosaurs kept this build, their short arms ending in three clawed fingers, though some had two or five. In the four-legged plant-eaters, arms evolved into stout props to support the body, yet they were usually shorter than the hindlegs. Most plant-eaters had four or five padded, blunt-nailed fingers that served as hooves; but in some dinosaurs the thumb ended in a long, sharp claw.

ARMS OF DEINOCHEIRUS

THE LONG ARM OF THE CLAW

Arms longer than a person, each tipped with vicious claws, are the only known fossils of *Deinocheirus* ("terrible hand"). Judging by its arms, this dinosaur was probably massive, but its true size and shape are a mystery – perhaps it was a midget with preposterously outsized limbs. Some scientists think it was a big-game hunter. Others think it hauled itself up trees like a sloth or used its arms to raid termites' nests.

POSSIBLE SIZE OF DEINOCHEIRUS COMPARED TO HUMAN

Deinonychus's *stiff tail was flexible at the base.*

DEINONYCHUS

Bony eye-ring

Fangs

Three-fingered hands

Toe-claw

VELOCIRAPTOR'S VICIOUS COUSIN

Twice as big as its cousin *Velociraptor*, *Deinonychus* was a powerful and agile hunter. It probably ran and leapt at prey, swinging its stiff tail to stay balanced during sudden movements. This mounted skeleton shows it pouncing, the clawed hands ready to grasp and the toe-claw ready to slash at the prey. A likely victim was *Tenontosaurus*, a plant-eater as big as a horse. At one fossil site, a *Tenontosaurus* was found with four *Deinonychus*. Perhaps the *Deinonychus* were members of a hunting pack that died during a violent battle.

Toe-claw

LETHAL WEAPONS

Deinonychus ("terrible claw") gets its name from the large, sickle-shaped toe-claws on its feet. Special muscles drew the claws back and then flicked them sharply down to slash through scaly skin and muscle. To avoid blunting these switchblade claws, they were held off the ground while walking.

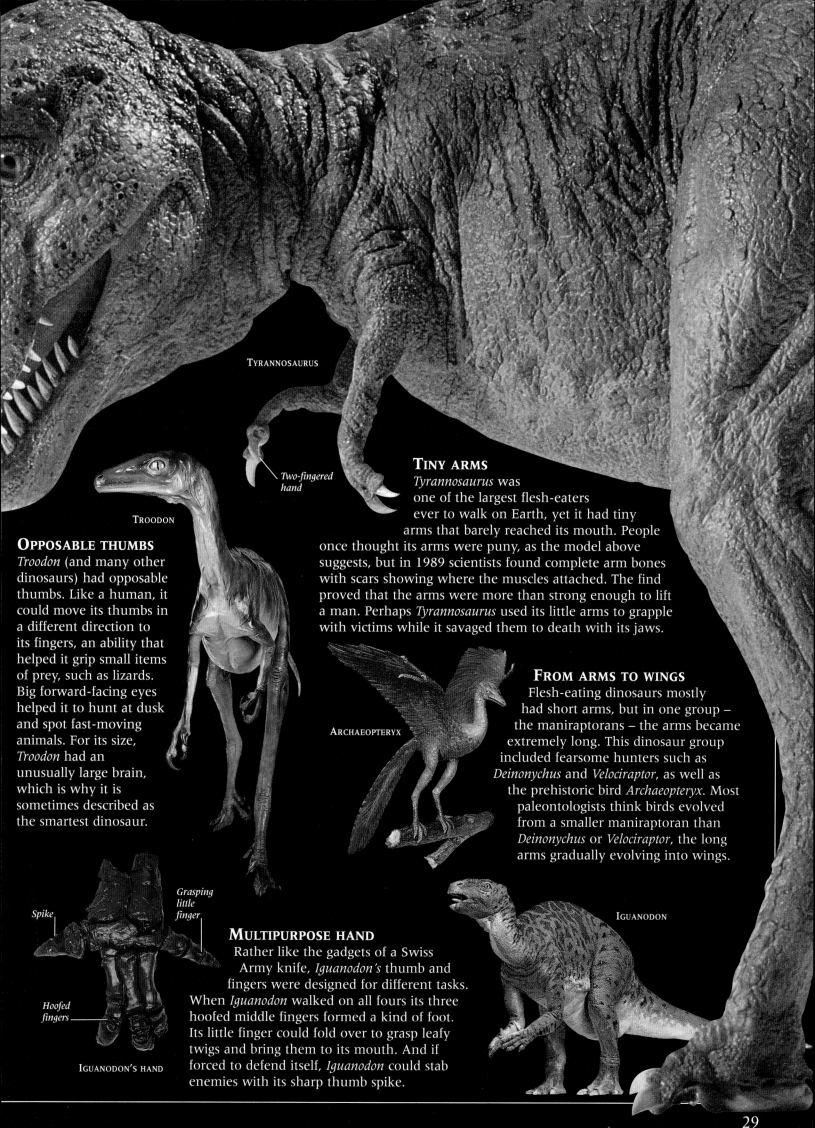

TYRANNOSAURUS

TROODON

Two-fingered hand

TINY ARMS

Tyrannosaurus was one of the largest flesh-eaters ever to walk on Earth, yet it had tiny arms that barely reached its mouth. People once thought its arms were puny, as the model above suggests, but in 1989 scientists found complete arm bones with scars showing where the muscles attached. The find proved that the arms were more than strong enough to lift a man. Perhaps *Tyrannosaurus* used its little arms to grapple with victims while it savaged them to death with its jaws.

OPPOSABLE THUMBS

Troodon (and many other dinosaurs) had opposable thumbs. Like a human, it could move its thumbs in a different direction to its fingers, an ability that helped it grip small items of prey, such as lizards. Big forward-facing eyes helped it to hunt at dusk and spot fast-moving animals. For its size, *Troodon* had an unusually large brain, which is why it is sometimes described as the smartest dinosaur.

ARCHAEOPTERYX

FROM ARMS TO WINGS

Flesh-eating dinosaurs mostly had short arms, but in one group – the maniraptorans – the arms became extremely long. This dinosaur group included fearsome hunters such as *Deinonychus* and *Velociraptor*, as well as the prehistoric bird *Archaeopteryx*. Most paleontologists think birds evolved from a smaller maniraptoran than *Deinonychus* or *Velociraptor*, the long arms gradually evolving into wings.

Grasping little finger

Spike

IGUANODON

MULTIPURPOSE HAND

Rather like the gadgets of a Swiss Army knife, *Iguanodon's* thumb and fingers were designed for different tasks. When *Iguanodon* walked on all fours its three hoofed middle fingers formed a kind of foot. Its little finger could fold over to grasp leafy twigs and bring them to its mouth. And if forced to defend itself, *Iguanodon* could stab enemies with its sharp thumb spike.

Hoofed fingers

IGUANODON'S HAND

KILLER INSTINCT

IMAGINE A MONSTER with teeth the size of daggers peering at you through an upstairs window. Lunging in, it snatches you in its immense jaws and swallows you whole. In the Age of Dinosaurs such creatures were no nightmare but terrible reality. The flesh-eating dinosaurs – theropods – evolved into giants because they had to tackle enormous prey. But as a result their prey became ever larger for protection. It is as if the flesh-eaters and plant-eaters became locked in an evolutionary "arms race," driving each other to immense sizes.

Teeth as sharp as carving knives lined the jaws.

GIGANTIC GIGANOTOSAURUS

Giganotosaurus may well have been the largest carnivore to walk the Earth. Weighing as much as 125 people, it was heavier and taller than *Tyrannosaurus*, though its brain was smaller. This monster terrorized the dinosaurs of South America 95 million years ago. One of its victims might have been the colossal sauropod *Argentinosaurus*, which weighed up to 100 tons. *Giganotosaurus* probably attacked it from the side, taking deep bites from its flanks. Even if the victim staggered off, it would probably have died from wounds infected by the rotting scraps of meat lodged between *Giganotosaurus's* fangs.

GIGANOTOSAURUS

TYRANNOSAURUS

GIGANOTOSAURUS

FOSSIL FINDS

TRIASSIC	JURASSIC	CRETACEOUS
248	205	144	65

Million years ago

Giganotosaurus's three-fingered hands were much bigger than those of Tyrannosaurus.

FAST OR SLOW?

In the film Jurassic Park, *Tyrannosaurus* races after a car, but could big theropods really run so fast? One scientist reckons *Tyrannosaurus's* leg bones were too weak to take the pounding of its 6-ton body when charging, limiting its top speed to about 16 mph (25 kmh). Other scientists think shock-absorbing tissue in its legs allowed a faster stride, perhaps up to 23 mph (36 kmh).

Powerful jaws were Tyrannosaurus's main weapon.

TYRANNOSAURUS REX

Tyrannosaurus attacked in a different way from *Giganotosaurus*. Holes found in victims' bones indicate that this predator's curved fangs punched deeply into flesh and bone. Then they pulled back, wrenching out huge mouthfuls of meat. The jaws and neck of *Tyrannosaurus* were tremendously powerful. It could pick up victims and shake them violently apart to kill them, before feasting on the dismembered corpse.

HUNTER OR SCAVENGER?

Some experts think *Tyrannosaurus* was a scavenger, feeding only on animals that were already dead. They claim it was too slow to capture live prey, but that the big smell center in its brain detected rotting flesh miles away. Perhaps *Tyrannosaurus* did eat ready-made corpses, but most scientists believe it was a hunter, too.

TYRANNOSAURUS

After gorging itself Tyrannosaurus would not need to hunt for days.

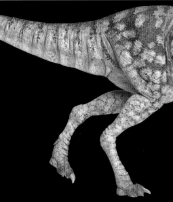

STRANGE DIETS

SCIENTISTS ONCE THOUGHT that all big flesh-eating dinosaurs ate only large plant-eating dinosaurs. Then fossil hunters discovered the spinosaurs – a group of large flesh-eaters with jaws and teeth made to eat sizable fish. There may have been other groups of dinosaurs with specialized diets, too. For instance, wide-mouthed dinosaurs may have been unfussy browsers, whereas narrow-mouthed plant-eaters probably chose what they ate.

SUCHOMIMUS

Using its curved thumb claws as meat hooks, Suchomimus could have scooped up unsuspecting fish.

OUT OF AFRICA
Fossil hunters discovered *Suchomimus's* remains in the Sahara in 1997. The team found the remains partly laid bare by desert winds, but removing the fossil bones still meant shifting 25 tons of rock and other material.

Suchomimus's name, meaning "crocodile mimic," comes from its long slender skull.

With its mouth full, Suchomimus *could still breathe, because its nostrils were behind the tip of its snout.*

SUCHOMIMUS
This bizarre fish-eating dinosaur grew as large as *Tyrannosaurus*. It had a head like a crocodile's, longer arms than most meat-eaters, and enormous hindlegs. Behind its head, tall spinal bones supported a skin fin, or maybe a tall, narrow hump, which ran down its back. *Suchomimus* probably waded out into rivers and lakes, then stood or lay in the water to catch big fish with its jaws or clawed hands.

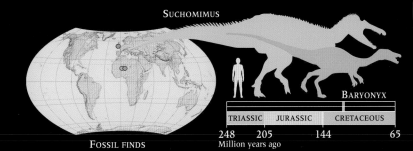

SUCHOMIMUS

BARYONYX

FOSSIL FINDS

TRIASSIC	JURASSIC		CRETACEOUS	
248	205	144		65

Million years ago

BARYONYX

CLOSE COUSINS?

Suchomimus from Niger was closely related to *Baryonyx*, a fish-eating dinosaur from England. *Suchomimus* may have evolved from relatives of *Baryonyx* that migrated from Europe to Africa when both places were joined, although scientists now think it possible that *Suchomimus* was just a big *Baryonyx*.

COELACANTH

FISH FOOD

It would have taken fleshy fish up to 13 ft (4 m) long to satisfy *Suchomimus's* appetite. Possible victims included a kind of prehistoric lungfish, or a fish called *Mawsonia*. "Living fossil" relatives of *Mawsonia*, known as coelacanths, can still be found in the ocean off East Africa and Southeast Asia.

FRIENDS OR FOES?

Today's crocodiles had prehistoric ancestors who lurked in the rivers where *Suchomimus* hunted. At 50 ft (15 m) long, the crocodilian *Sarcosuchus* was even larger than *Suchomimus*. Both kinds of reptile had narrow heads and slender, sharp teeth to cope with slippery prey. Sometimes, perhaps, dinosaur and crocodilian fought over a fish. The result would have been a bloodthirsty battle.

Crocodiles have changed very little since prehistoric times.

DIVIDING THE SPOILS

COELOPHYSIS WAS AS LONG AS A CAR but as light as an 8-year-old child. In the late Triassic, gangs of this bloodthirsty, birdlike dinosaur swarmed through semi-deserts and riverside forests, snapping up small game. Working together, a pack would have made light work of animals much larger than themselves. Prehistoric reptiles called aetosaurs were probably too well-armored to kill, but if a pack of *Coelophysis* found one dead, their sharp little teeth would have quickly reduced the corpse to a skeleton as they squabbled over the remains.

NIMBLE PREDATOR

Slim and agile, *Coelophysis* was built for darting after prey at speed. In many ways it was similar to long-legged water birds of today, such as storks and herons. Its narrow head, S-shaped neck, slender body, long legs, and hollow bones were much like a bird's. So, too, were other features of its skeleton. But *Coelophysis* had a bony tail, clawed hands, not wings, and sharp little teeth instead of a beak.

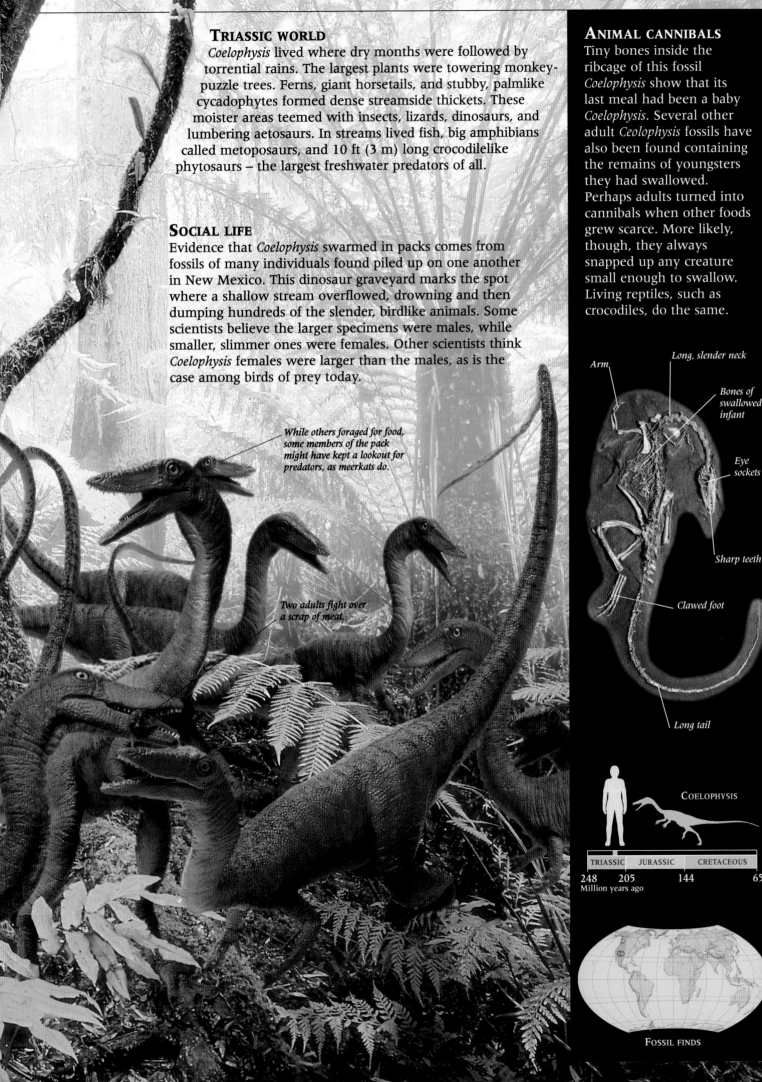

TRIASSIC WORLD

Coelophysis lived where dry months were followed by torrential rains. The largest plants were towering monkey-puzzle trees. Ferns, giant horsetails, and stubby, palmlike cycadophytes formed dense streamside thickets. These moister areas teemed with insects, lizards, dinosaurs, and lumbering aetosaurs. In streams lived fish, big amphibians called metoposaurs, and 10 ft (3 m) long crocodilelike phytosaurs – the largest freshwater predators of all.

SOCIAL LIFE

Evidence that *Coelophysis* swarmed in packs comes from fossils of many individuals found piled up on one another in New Mexico. This dinosaur graveyard marks the spot where a shallow stream overflowed, drowning and then dumping hundreds of the slender, birdlike animals. Some scientists believe the larger specimens were males, while smaller, slimmer ones were females. Other scientists think *Coelophysis* females were larger than the males, as is the case among birds of prey today.

While others foraged for food, some members of the pack might have kept a lookout for predators, as meerkats do.

Two adults fight over a scrap of meat.

ANIMAL CANNIBALS

Tiny bones inside the ribcage of this fossil *Coelophysis* show that its last meal had been a baby *Coelophysis*. Several other adult *Ceolophysis* fossils have also been found containing the remains of youngsters they had swallowed. Perhaps adults turned into cannibals when other foods grew scarce. More likely, though, they always snapped up any creature small enough to swallow. Living reptiles, such as crocodiles, do the same.

Arm

Long, slender neck

Bones of swallowed infant

Eye sockets

Sharp teeth

Clawed foot

Long tail

COELOPHYSIS

TRIASSIC	JURASSIC	CRETACEOUS
248 205		144 65

Million years ago

FOSSIL FINDS

A TAIL OF DEFENSE

Dinosaurs led dangerous lives. Predators, rivals, parasites, diseases, and injuries would have killed off most before they grew old. The deadliest threats were the fangs and claws of big predators like *Tyrannosaurus*. Most dinosaurs were too big to burrow or climb, so they relied on other kinds of protection from these killers. Hatchlings may have stayed in thick vegetation, perhaps using camouflage to hide. Ostrich dinosaurs outran their attackers, and ankylosaurs were protected by body armor. Many plant-eating dinosaurs probably found safety in numbers by living in herds. The sauropods – the biggest animals ever to walk on Earth – relied for defense on their sheer weight and size, which made them dangerous to attack. When this failed, some may have used a secret weapon: a whiplash tail.

WHIPLASH

Barosaurus, like many other sauropods, had a huge, muscular tail that it might have been able to flick like a whip. Movable joints between the bones in the tail allowed it to bend freely from side to side. If a large predator approached from behind, *Barosaurus* could have cracked its whiplash tail with savage force, smashing the attacker in the face. Some scientists think male sauropods may have engaged in whip-cracking contests as they fought over mates.

SAUROPOD HERDS

Fossilized footprints provide strong evidence that sauropods lived in herds. Tracks found on a ranch in Texas, USA, appeared to have been made by 23 dinosaurs traveling together; the smaller prints overlapped the larger ones, implying that the largest animals led the herd. Other track discoveries show where sauropod herds walked in single file, or side by side in a massive row.

If Barosaurus *whipped its tail, the tip would have traveled faster than the speed of sound, making a loud crack as it crossed the sound barrier.*

FOSSIL FINDS

ALLOSAURUS
BAROSAURUS

TRIASSIC	JURASSIC	CRETACEOUS

248   205   144   65
Million years ago

PROTECTIVE PARENTS?

Young, old, and sick sauropods would have been most at risk from attack. Some experts think the youngest sauropods stayed in the middle of the herd for safety. Others think that mothers abandoned their eggs after laying them, leaving the young to fend for themselves. After hatching out, the tiny youngsters might have run for cover in thick forest, where they could hide from big predators. Only when they grew large would they join a herd.

ALLOSAURUS

The most dangerous enemy that *Barosaurus* was likely to face was the theropod *Allosaurus*. This huge flesh-eater may have hunted in packs to bring down big game. Even a fully grown *Barosaurus* would have collapsed if a squad of these monsters attacked from all sides.

BATTERING RAMS

Another sauropod defensive tactic could have been to use the front limbs as battering rams. Rearing on its hindlegs to face an attacker, *Barosaurus* might have raised its forefeet high above a big theropod's head. If the predator moved in to savage its belly, *Barosaurus* could have brought these stubby "hands" crashing down on the theropod's back, with the great weight of its body behind them. Sauropods also had sharp thumb-claws to gouge nasty wounds in an enemy's hide.

FROM HEAD TO TAIL

DINOSAURS, LIKE HUMANS, belong to a group of animals called vertebrates. The key feature of all vertebrates is the spine – a stiff rod made up of small bones running from the head to the tail. The spines of dinosaurs reveal a great deal about the way they moved. In some dinosaurs, the bones of the spine were joined by flexible joints, allowing these dinosaurs to swing their necks and tails at will. In others, rodlike stiffeners made parts of the spine rigid. The rear part of the spine formed the tail, which provided vital balance and sometimes formed a special weapon for self-defense.

GRAZERS' NECKS

By comparing the necks of plant-eating dinosaurs like *Parasaurolophus* and animals today, we can guess how they fed. *Parasaurolophus's* neck curved sharply like a bison's. Bison bend their necks to eat ground plants like grass, so *Parasaurolophus* may also have browsed at ground level. There was no grass in the dinosaur era, so it probably ate ferns and early flowering plants.

Parasaurolophus had a sharply curved neck like a bison's.

PARASAUROLOPHUS

Flesh-eating dinosaurs tended to have an S-shaped neck.

TAILS FOR AGILITY

Unusual tails helped *Dromaeosaurus* and its close relative *Velociraptor* produce the sudden turns that made their swift attacks so deadly. Most of the tail bones were locked together by special bony rods to form a stiff bar; only where the tail met the hips was it free to move around. This combination of stiffness and flexibility allowed these predators to raise and swing their tails in any direction. Balancing like acrobats, they could turn at high speed and twist in midair while leaping to strike a victim.

DROMAEOSAURUS

Dromaeosaurus *was about 6 ft (1.8 m) long – about the same size as* Velociraptor. *Like* Velociraptor, *this animal was a rapacious predator.*

The large back claw flicked forwards as Dromaeosaurus *kicked at its prey.*

The sickle-shaped claws were used to slash through skin.

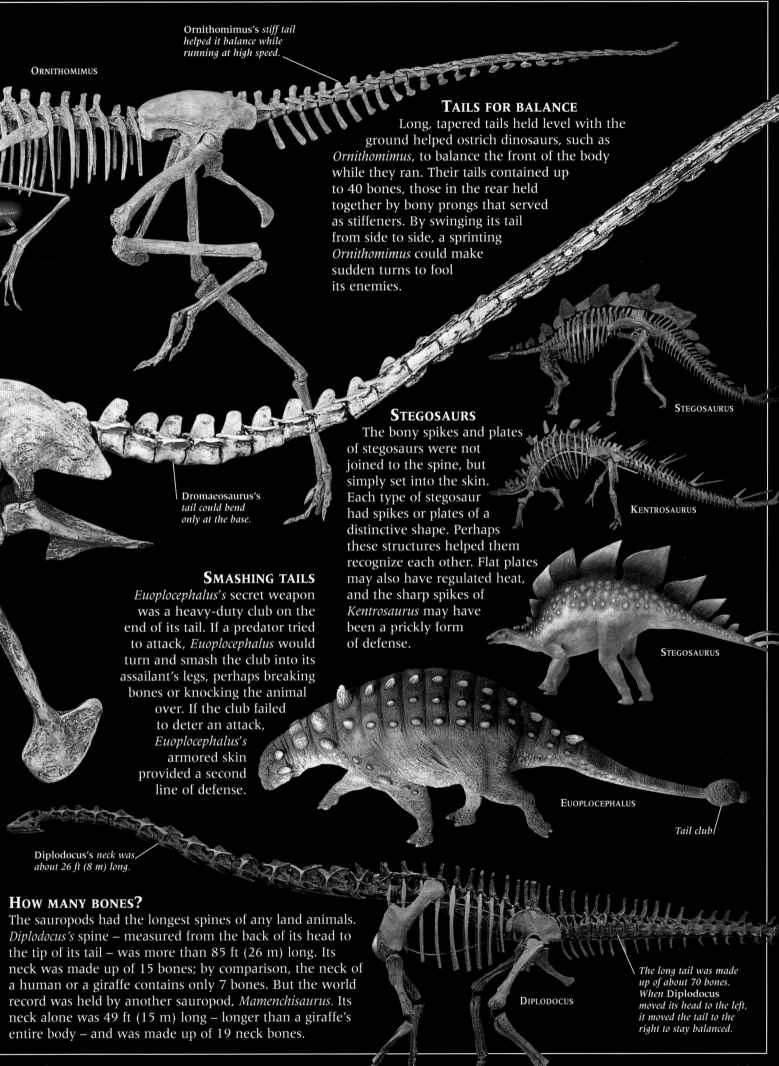

ORNITHOMIMUS

Ornithomimus's *stiff tail helped it balance while running at high speed.*

TAILS FOR BALANCE

Long, tapered tails held level with the ground helped ostrich dinosaurs, such as *Ornithomimus*, to balance the front of the body while they ran. Their tails contained up to 40 bones, those in the rear held together by bony prongs that served as stiffeners. By swinging its tail from side to side, a sprinting *Ornithomimus* could make sudden turns to fool its enemies.

STEGOSAURUS

STEGOSAURS

The bony spikes and plates of stegosaurs were not joined to the spine, but simply set into the skin. Each type of stegosaur had spikes or plates of a distinctive shape. Perhaps these structures helped them recognize each other. Flat plates may also have regulated heat, and the sharp spikes of *Kentrosaurus* may have been a prickly form of defense.

KENTROSAURUS

Dromaeosaurus's tail could bend only at the base.

SMASHING TAILS

Euoplocephalus's secret weapon was a heavy-duty club on the end of its tail. If a predator tried to attack, *Euoplocephalus* would turn and smash the club into its assailant's legs, perhaps breaking bones or knocking the animal over. If the club failed to deter an attack, *Euoplocephalus's* armored skin provided a second line of defense.

STEGOSAURUS

EUOPLOCEPHALUS

Tail club

Diplodocus's *neck was about 26 ft (8 m) long.*

HOW MANY BONES?

The sauropods had the longest spines of any land animals. *Diplodocus's* spine – measured from the back of its head to the tip of its tail – was more than 85 ft (26 m) long. Its neck was made up of 15 bones; by comparison, the neck of a human or a giraffe contains only 7 bones. But the world record was held by another sauropod, *Mamenchisaurus*. Its neck alone was 49 ft (15 m) long – longer than a giraffe's entire body – and was made up of 19 neck bones.

DIPLODOCUS

The long tail was made up of about 70 bones. When Diplodocus *moved its head to the left, it moved the tail to the right to stay balanced.*

SUITS OF ARMOR

CANNED FOOD ONLY MAKES a meal if you have a can opener. To a flesh-eating dinosaur, armored prey were like walking meals that were impossible to get at because of the studs, plates, and spikes that protected them. These suits of armor enabled their plant-eating owners to outwit predators for tens of millions of years. During that time, the armored dinosaurs evolved from small, lightweight species with just a few rows of studs on their backs into huge lumbering beasts as heavy as elephants and shielded like battle tanks.

SUIT OF SPIKES

Gastonia (right) was a walking fortress as long as a racquetball court is wide. Short legs and a low build kept its body close to the ground, protecting its belly from attack. Large bony spikes stuck out from its shoulders and ran down its back and tail, protecting the upper body. So much for its passive defenses; *Gastonia* could also counterattack by swinging its armored tail violently to the side. Such defenses were vital to this herbivore, because it lived at the same time as *Utahraptor*, a savage predator built like *Velociraptor* but twice its size.

Ferns were abundant in Gastonia's time, but their tough fibrous stems might have made them difficult to digest.

FAVORITE FOOD

Gastonia held its head low and so could eat only plants at ground level or just above. Most likely, it cropped the soft, fleshy "flowers" of some seed-ferns – prehistoric plants with fernlike fronds that sprouted from stubby tree trunks. Horsetails and ferns were probably plentiful, but their stems might have been too tough for *Gastonia's* teeth.

EDMONTONIA

Edmontonia resembled a gigantic, prickly armadillo. Bands of thorny plates ran across its back and tail, and large bony spikes shielded its neck and shoulders. Its skull was protected by smaller plates of bone that fitted together like a jigsaw puzzle. A big carnivore might have tried overturning *Edmontonia* to attack its soft underbelly. But *Edmontonia* could fight back by charging at the attacker and stabbing its shoulder spikes into their flesh.

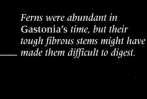

Shoulder spike

Flank spike

Armored tail

EDMONTONIA

Stocky legs

CHAIN MAIL

These two photographs show a fossil *Sauropelta* from above and below. *Sauropelta's* back (top) was covered with bony cones and smaller bony studs. These formed a flexible armor that let it move around freely, like a knight in chain mail. But its soft belly (bottom) was less well defended and it might have had to crouch during an attack.

Bony stud

Bony cone

SAUROPELTA

Spine

Ribs

FOSSIL FINDS

GASTONIA   EDMONTONIA

TRIASSIC	JURASSIC	CRETACEOUS

248   205   144   65
Million years ago

COLOR AND CAMOUFLAGE

NOBODY KNOWS HOW ANY DINOSAUR was colored. Pigments, the coloring ingredients in skin, rarely survive with fossil bones. But at least we can make sensible guesses. Our best clues come from living relatives of dinosaurs – birds and crocodiles – and from animals that resemble them in size or lifestyle, such as large mammals. From these it seems likely that many dinosaurs had camouflage: patterns and colors to help them hide from enemies. Brightly colored skins or crests may have helped some dinosaurs to scare off rivals or win a mate. Perhaps only the biggest dinosaurs were as drab as elephants, their vast size making camouflage unnecessary.

BLENDING IN

Like green birds or lizards, big dinosaurs with green scaly skin would have been invisible standing still in a thicket of ferns. If *Iguanodon* was green, a whole herd munching leaves might have escaped detection by the predators that prowled their swampy forest home. Young *Iguanodon*s may have had the brightest colors, fading as they aged, as happens in some lizards today.

VELOCIRAPTOR

Tiger stripes?

DEADLY DISGUISES

With the agile, predatory lifestyle of a cat, *Velociraptor* might have had catlike camouflage to help it hide while it crept up on prey. Tigers have black stripes to hide in grass, but there was no grass in *Velociraptor's* time so this pattern seems unlikely. Lizardlike green skin is even more far-fetched because *Velociraptor* lived in a desert and vegetation was sparse. A more likely possibility is pale skin with dark blotches, like a leopard. A light, dusty color would have matched the surroundings, and spots would have broken up its outline and helped it hide in dappled shade under shrubs.

Green like a lizard?

Or spotted like a leopard?

IGUANODON

FOSSIL FINDS

TRIASSIC	JURASSIC	CRETACEOUS
248	205	144	65

Million years ago

*Forests of tree ferns were
a common sight during
the Age of Dinosaurs.
Today, these prehistoric
plants survive in only
a few remote locations
untouched by humans.*

PEACEFUL VEGETARIAN

Iguanodon was a peaceful
plant-eater, with a long head
like a horse's and hands that
pulled leafy stems to its
mouth. As heavy as a female
elephant, it ran or walked on
its hindlegs and could also
amble on all fours. Apart
from camouflage, its best
defense against large
theropods would be
hurrying away or
stabbing an attacker
with its spiky thumb.

WINNING A MATE

A MONG BIRDS, mammals, and reptiles, the biggest, strongest, or most colorful male often has the best chance of winning a mate. So it must have been among the dinosaurs. In the mating season, males would have tested their strength against one another, showing off their crests, horns, or bright colors. Perhaps some engaged in violent battles, fighting to the death. The strongest or showiest males would have won the chance to mate with a female. By choosing the winning males, the females were choosing the best genes to pass on to their offspring.

JOUSTING MATCH

The battle for supremacy between male *Pentaceratops* must have been a remarkable sight. Facing one another, they probably dipped their heads to brandish their fearsome horns and show off their massive frills. Perhaps they locked horns and wrestled. Eventually, a loser would break away, lower his head, and slink off. The winner might have celebrated by snorting and pawing the ground.

ATTRACTIVE COLORS

Pentaceratops may have used its frill to impress females, much as a peacock spreads its tail or a male bird of paradise flashes its bright feathers. The colors and energetic courtship displays of these male birds tell females that they are healthy and in good breeding condition. The color of a male *Pentaceratops's* frill is a mystery, but perhaps it too was decorative to attract females, or perhaps, like a peacock's tail, it sported startling "eyespots" to attract attention.

BIRD OF PARADISE

STAGS FIGHTING

BATTLING MALES

Our notions of how the horned dinosaurs used their frills and horns come partly from the rutting behavior of deer. Male deer (stags) grow huge antlers that attract females (does). Rival males lock antlers and try to shove each other backward. The one losing ground eventually runs away and the winner mates with a herd of does.

FANTASTIC FRILL

The frill of *Pentaceratops* was nearly 3 ft (1 m) wide. To keep it lightweight, there were huge empty "windows" in the bone, covered with skin. These windows make it unlikely that the frill could have been used for protection or to anchor muscles.

PENTACERATOPS

TRIASSIC	JURASSIC	CRETACEOUS

248   205   144   65
Million years ago

FOSSIL FINDS

FIVE-HORNED FACE

Pentaceratops means "five-horned face," but this dinosaur really had three horns: two long ones over the eyes and a short nose horn. Its other "horns" were just pointed cheek bones. All horned dinosaurs had these, but in *Pentaceratops* they were exceptionally long. Its "parrot's beak" was used to grasp and tear off mouthfuls of twigs and leaves. Batteries of self-sharpening teeth in the mouth meant it could cope easily with the toughest vegetation.

HEADS AND SKULLS

LIKE YOURS, A DINOSAUR'S SKULL protected its brain and housed organs for sight, smell, and hearing as well as its airways, jaws, and teeth. Most dinosaur skulls had "windows" to save weight or take jaw muscles, but there was a great range of sizes and shapes. Sauropods, the largest dinosaurs, had heads no bigger than those of horses, yet the much smaller horned dinosaurs had skulls up to 10 ft (3 m) long – the largest heads of any land animal. But even the biggest dinosaur skulls housed brains with a tiny cerebrum, the thinking part.

CARNIVORES' HEADS

Huge windows lightened *Allosaurus's* 3 ft (1 m) long skull, leaving holes for the eyes, ears, nostrils, and jaw muscles. Sharp hearing and a keen sense of smell helped this gigantic carnivore find its victims. Like other big meat-eaters, it had massive jaws operated by powerful muscles. To swallow large mouthfuls, special joints in the skull let the jaws open extra wide.

BRACHYLOPHOSAURUS

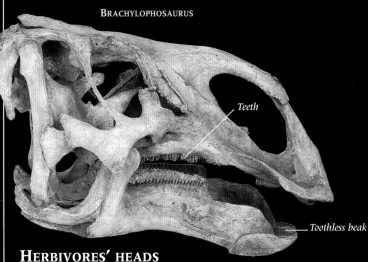

Teeth

Toothless beak

ALLOSAURUS

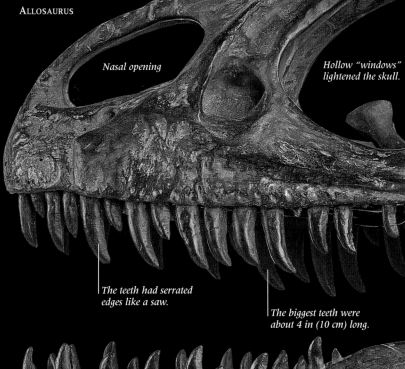

Nasal opening

Hollow "windows" lightened the skull.

The teeth had serrated edges like a saw.

The biggest teeth were about 4 in (10 cm) long.

HERBIVORES' HEADS

Plant-eating dinosaurs' heads were geared to eating vegetation. For instance, the hadrosaur *Brachylophosaurus* had a toothless beak for cropping leaves, and hundreds of sharp, close-packed cheek teeth. Shutting its mouth pushed the upper jaws apart, making the upper teeth slide over lower teeth to grind up food. In contrast, the tall sauropods simply swallowed their food and allowed swallowed stones in the stomach to grind it up.

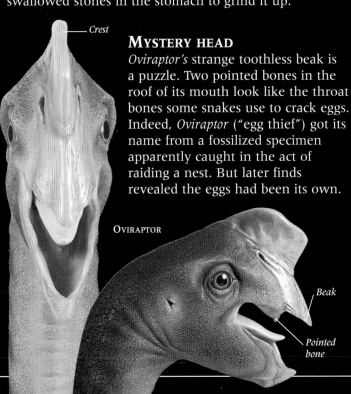

Crest

MYSTERY HEAD

Oviraptor's strange toothless beak is a puzzle. Two pointed bones in the roof of its mouth look like the throat bones some snakes use to crack eggs. Indeed, *Oviraptor* ("egg thief") got its name from a fossilized specimen apparently caught in the act of raiding a nest. But later finds revealed the eggs had been its own.

OVIRAPTOR

Beak

Pointed bone

CROCODILE TEETH

Suchomimus had a long, narrow head like a crocodile's, and teeth to match. While other meat-eaters' teeth were sharp, flat-sided blades, those of *Suchomimus* were more like the pointed prongs of a rake. This African dinosaur's teeth were designed to grip slippery prey – probably fish.

Curved jaws

Sharp teeth like a crocodile's.

SUCHOMIMUS

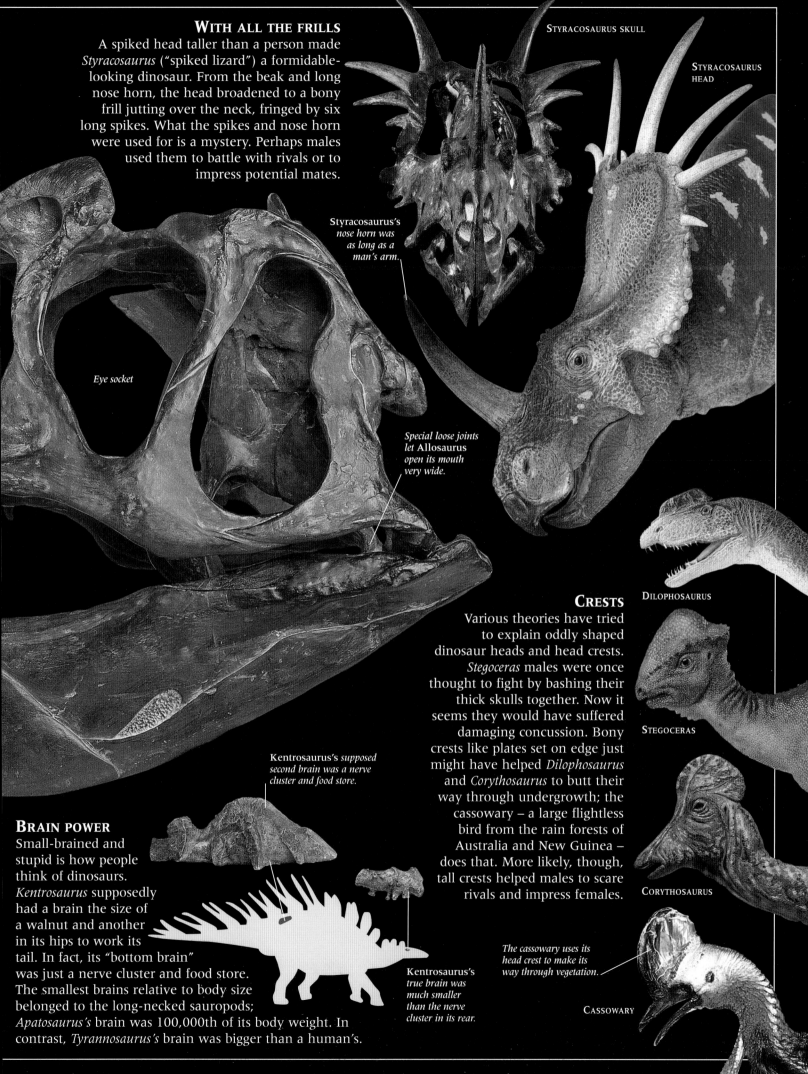

WITH ALL THE FRILLS

A spiked head taller than a person made *Styracosaurus* ("spiked lizard") a formidable-looking dinosaur. From the beak and long nose horn, the head broadened to a bony frill jutting over the neck, fringed by six long spikes. What the spikes and nose horn were used for is a mystery. Perhaps males used them to battle with rivals or to impress potential mates.

STYRACOSAURUS SKULL

STYRACOSAURUS HEAD

Styracosaurus's nose horn was as long as a man's arm.

Eye socket

Special loose joints let Allosaurus open its mouth very wide.

DILOPHOSAURUS

CRESTS

Various theories have tried to explain oddly shaped dinosaur heads and head crests. *Stegoceras* males were once thought to fight by bashing their thick skulls together. Now it seems they would have suffered damaging concussion. Bony crests like plates set on edge just might have helped *Dilophosaurus* and *Corythosaurus* to butt their way through undergrowth; the cassowary – a large flightless bird from the rain forests of Australia and New Guinea – does that. More likely, though, tall crests helped males to scare rivals and impress females.

STEGOCERAS

Kentrosaurus's supposed second brain was a nerve cluster and food store.

CORYTHOSAURUS

BRAIN POWER

Small-brained and stupid is how people think of dinosaurs. *Kentrosaurus* supposedly had a brain the size of a walnut and another in its hips to work its tail. In fact, its "bottom brain" was just a nerve cluster and food store. The smallest brains relative to body size belonged to the long-necked sauropods; *Apatosaurus's* brain was 100,000th of its body weight. In contrast, *Tyrannosaurus's* brain was bigger than a human's.

Kentrosaurus's true brain was much smaller than the nerve cluster in its rear.

The cassowary uses its head crest to make its way through vegetation.

CASSOWARY

EXTRAORDINARY EGGS

FOSSILIZED DINOSAUR EGGS HAVE BEEN FOUND all over the world, sometimes in vast numbers. One Spanish site holds 300,000. These were probably laid at a mass-breeding ground that dinosaurs returned to each year. There are about 40 different kinds of dinosaur egg, from "cannonballs" and "long loaves" to tiny eggs that would fit in your hand. Like birds' eggs, they all had hard shells. A few contain babies' bones, clues to the kind of dinosaur that laid them. Fossilized mud nests with the remains of hatchlings help to solve another puzzle: did dinosaur mothers abandon their eggs as lizards and turtles do, or nurture them as birds and crocodiles do?

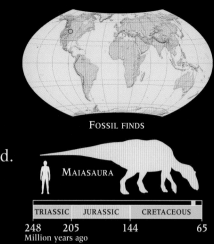

FOSSIL FINDS

MAIASAURA

TRIASSIC	JURASSIC	CRETACEOUS
248	205	144	65

Million years ago

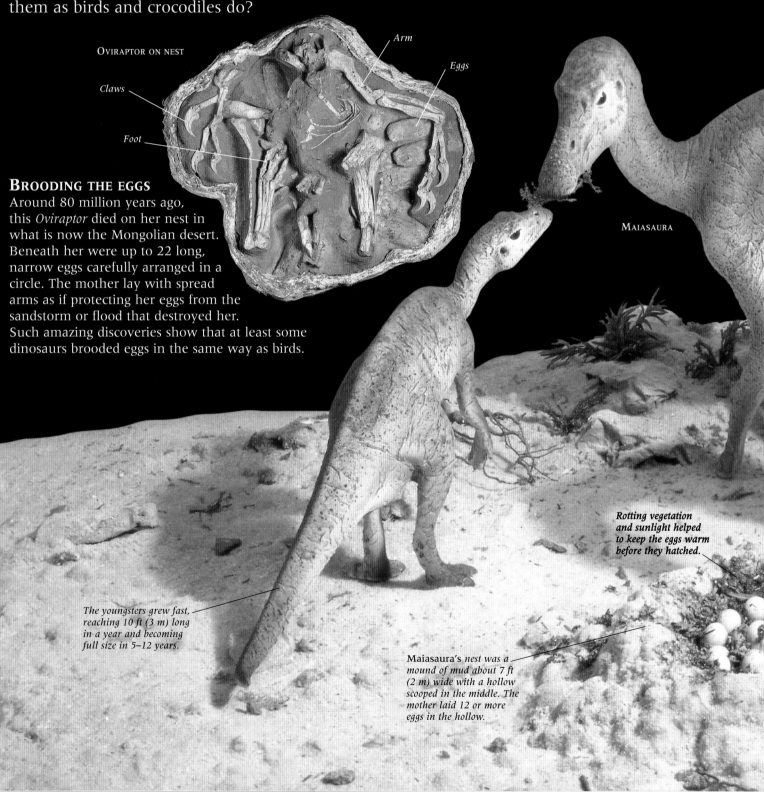

OVIRAPTOR ON NEST

Arm

Eggs

Claws

Foot

BROODING THE EGGS

Around 80 million years ago, this *Oviraptor* died on her nest in what is now the Mongolian desert. Beneath her were up to 22 long, narrow eggs carefully arranged in a circle. The mother lay with spread arms as if protecting her eggs from the sandstorm or flood that destroyed her. Such amazing discoveries show that at least some dinosaurs brooded eggs in the same way as birds.

MAIASAURA

Rotting vegetation and sunlight helped to keep the eggs warm before they hatched.

The youngsters grew fast, reaching 10 ft (3 m) long in a year and becoming full size in 5–12 years.

Maiasaura's nest was a mound of mud about 7 ft (2 m) wide with a hollow scooped in the middle. The mother laid 12 or more eggs in the hollow.

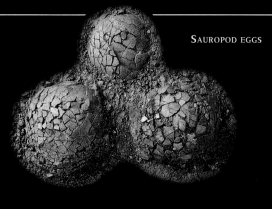

SAUROPOD EGGS

HATCHING OUT

These dinosaur hatchling models were based on tiny bones and eggs dug up at Egg Mountain, a dinosaur site in Montana. Experts believed they had found nests of *Orodromeus*, a small plant-eating dinosaur; but closer study showed the embryos and eggs were those of *Troodon*, a flesh-eater. *Troodon* had seemingly nested in groups, the mothers brooding their eggs. Perhaps *Orodromeus* bones found among the nests were remains of *Troodon's* meals.

A hatchling takes its first look at the outside world.

Baby Troodons *were about as big as gerbils.*

EGG SIZES

The biggest dinosaurs – sauropods – laid surprisingly small eggs. A 30-ton female laid eggs no more than 11 lb (5 kg) in weight – about one six-thousandth of her own weight. At only 30 times lighter than a chicken, a hen's egg is huge in comparison.

INSIDE AN EGG

This rare find is a dinosaur egg containing the tiny bones of an unhatched embryo. The egg is only about 3 in (7 cm) wide, yet the baby inside would have grown into an adult *Oviraptor* 6 ft 6 in (2 m) long. In the same nest was the skull of another dinosaur, perhaps food brought by the mother.

OVIRAPTOR EGG

GOOD MOTHER LIZARD

Maiasaura ("good mother lizard") earned its name from finds of mud nests in Montana, where this big, duck-billed dinosaur laid eggs and tended its young. Many mud nests lay close together, showing that the dinosaurs nested in colonies for protection from predators, much as seabirds do today. One nest held a number of nestlings whose legs seemed too weak to walk around. Scientists suspect these helpless nestlings must have depended on their parents to bring them food.

Newly hatched Maiasaura *babies were about as long as a human foot. They stayed in the nest until they were at least 3 ft (1 m) long.*

END OF AN ERA

ABOUT 75 MILLION YEARS AGO there were more kinds of dinosaur than ever; yet 10 million years later all but the birds had vanished. Indeed, no land animal heavier than a large dog survived. Also gone were the pterosaurs and many sea creatures. At least 80 theories have tried to explain how so much life was wiped off the face of the Earth. Most are absurd – no one still thinks that dinosaurs became too large to breed, for instance. But experts argue to this day about what must have happened. Although it is hard to tell from fossil evidence how quickly the mass extinction took place, many scientists suspect it was caused by a sudden catastrophe, such as a massive comet or asteroid collision.

LAST OF THE DINOSAURS

This remarkable fossil of the duck-billed dinosaur *Edmontosaurus* shows it apparently curled up as it was when it died in the late Cretaceous. *Edmontosaurus* was one of the species that survived right up to the end of the Cretaceous; then it mysteriously vanished. Studies of the fossil record reveal that, just after *Edmontosaurus* and the other dinosaurs disappeared, ferns became suddenly common. Perhaps these plants were spreading to recolonize a devastated landscape.

The asteroid or comet that made the Chicxulub crater hit Earth with a force 10,000 times greater than all the world's nuclear bombs put together.

USA

Gulf of Mexico

MEXICO

CHICXULUB CRATER

Pacific Ocean

The crater now lies buried under 3,600 ft (1,100 m) of rock, formed over millions of years from sea sediments. Few clues to the crater's presence remain at the surface.

Soon after its formation, the Chicxulub crater might have been visible as a massive circle of mountains. Sixty-five million years of weathering have now leveled the mountains and sea sediments have filled in the crater.

DEEP IMPACT

In the early 1990s, geologists discovered a 112 mile (180 km) wide crater in Mexico. It seems to have formed when a comet or asteroid smashed into Earth 65 million years ago – exactly when the dinosaurs disappeared. The impact would have been phenomenal. Vast clouds of rock and dust would have filled the atmosphere, hiding the Sun. Maybe the dinosaurs died out during the dark, freezing months that resulted from this catastrophe.

This slab of limestone is made entirely of ammonite shells. Ammonites were octopuslike animals that lived in coiled shells, their tentacles waving out of the open end to capture prey.

AMMONITE

DEATH IN THE OCEANS

Whatever catastrophe destroyed the dinosaurs 65 million years ago also caused mass extinction in the seas. The casualties included plesiosaurs, ammonites and belemnites (both relatives of octopuses), certain fish, and tiny chalk-forming single-celled organisms. Ichthyosaurs and sea crocodiles had vanished already, perhaps outcompeted by sharks.

VOLCANOES

When the Chicxulub impact happened, dinosaurs were probably already suffering the effects of huge volcanic eruptions in India. For thousands of years, cracks in the ground oozed lava that piled up miles thick across an area as large as Alaska and Texas combined. Dust and ash thrown into the sky might have screened out the Sun and changed the planet's climate.

Volcanic eruptions can launch huge amounts of ash, dust, and rock fragments into the sky.

Shockwaves after impact might have given the crater two rims.

ARTIST'S IMPRESSION OF THE CHICXULUB CRATER

DINOBIRDS

IN 1861 AN ASTONISHING FOSSIL turned up in a German quarry. It was a beautifully preserved skeleton of a creature almost identical to the midget dinosaur *Compsognathus*, except for one shocking difference: it had feathers. This animal, called *Archaeopteryx*, is now thought to have been a halfway stage in the evolution of birds from small predatory dinosaurs. So perhaps dinosaurs were not wiped out after all, and now live all around us. Some scientists disagree with this theory, but paleontologists have recently found more feathered "dinobirds," making the line between dinosaurs and birds ever more blurred.

DINOTURKEY

Turkey-sized *Caudipteryx* (right), whose discovery was announced in 1998, seems to have been both a bird and a dinosaur. Downy feathers covered its body, and long feathers sprouted from its arms and fan-shaped tail; yet its "wings" were too small for flight. Its skull, hips, and feet were like those of a predatory dinosaur and, unlike modern birds, it had teeth and clawed hands. *Caudipteryx* was less birdlike than *Archaeopteryx*, but it lived much later. This suggests it was a flightless descendant of early dinobirds, rather than a dinosaur that was turning into a bird.

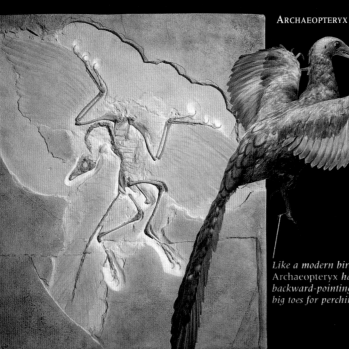

ARCHAEOPTERYX

Like a modern bird, Archaeopteryx had backward-pointing big toes for perching.

ARCHAEOPTERYX

Despite its teeth and bony tail, *Archaeopteryx* was clearly a bird, as it had wings fringed with long flight feathers exactly like those of birds today. The shafts of its feathers were off center, a feature that helps to generate lift during flight. But its shallow breastbone indicates that *Archaeopteryx*'s flapping muscles were weak. It could probably take only short, low gliding flights around the desert islands it inhabited.

IN A FLAP

Although it could not fly, *Caudipteryx* probably had other uses for its wings. Perhaps they helped it swoop to the ground from trees. Or perhaps it flapped them and fanned its tail to intimidate rivals or attract mates, as birds do today. *Caudipteryx* probably pecked up plant foods of various kinds and ground them down between stones in its stomach. Its long legs would have made it a very fast runner.

Hoatzins live in the rain forests of South America.

GROUND UP OR TREE DOWN?

Hoatzins are unusual birds that have claws on their wings when young. Hatchlings use these to clamber about in trees. Some people think the first birds clawed their way up tree trunks like this, then fluttered down. Others believe that flight first began as they ran after prey, flapping their feathered arms to gain speed.

WAS VELOCIRAPTOR A DINOBIRD?

Velociraptor had many characteristics in common with *Archaeopteryx*. Its

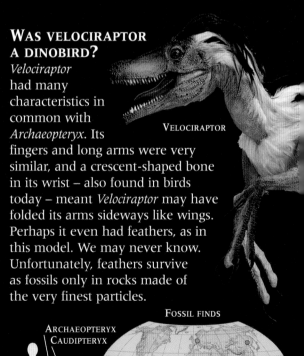

VELOCIRAPTOR

fingers and long arms were very similar, and a crescent-shaped bone in its wrist – also found in birds today – meant *Velociraptor* may have folded its arms sideways like wings. Perhaps it even had feathers, as in this model. We may never know. Unfortunately, feathers survive as fossils only in rocks made of the very finest particles.

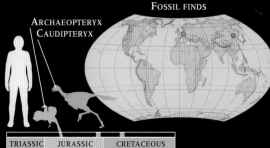

FOSSIL FINDS

ARCHAEOPTERYX
CAUDIPTERYX

TRIASSIC	JURASSIC	CRETACEOUS	
248	205	144	65

Million years ago

FOSSILS

W E KNOW SO MUCH about dinosaurs thanks to fossil remains of their bodies, footprints, and droppings in rocks that were once sand or mud. Fossils include teeth, mineral-hardened bones, and hollows (molds) left by footprints or bones that dissolved. Perhaps only one dinosaur in a million was fossilized, and far fewer left whole skeletons. The rest vanished completely – eaten, rotted away, or eroded by weather. But some finds are truly spectacular. They include fossils of dinosaurs fighting when smothered by sandstorms, and whole herds drowned by floods.

DINOSAUR CORPSE

A museum model of fish-eating *Baryonyx* shows how the dinosaur lay when it died. About 124 million years ago this large animal sank to the floor of a lake, where its corpse lay undisturbed. Although the flesh decayed, protective mud covered its bones. Working with scientists, a model-maker was able to show what *Baryonyx* looked like when muscles and skin still covered its body.

COMPSOGNATHUS

Hand

These two dinosaurs lived near a river 150 million years ago.

One has died, its flesh has rotted away, and its skeleton lies on a dried river bed.

The skeleton is buried by mud and river sediment, and the bones become as hard as rock over millions of years.

Today the rock that contains the fossilized dinosaur has come to the surface and is being eroded. Scientists have found the animal's remains.

HOW FOSSILS FORM

In order for a skeleton to be fossilized before it decomposes, it must be buried quickly, for instance by windblown sand or mud washed into a river. Over millions of years the sand or mud turn into rock. Water trickling through the ground deposits minerals inside pores in the bones, making them harden. But if water or scavengers scattered the bones before burial, experts will find it difficult to put them back together

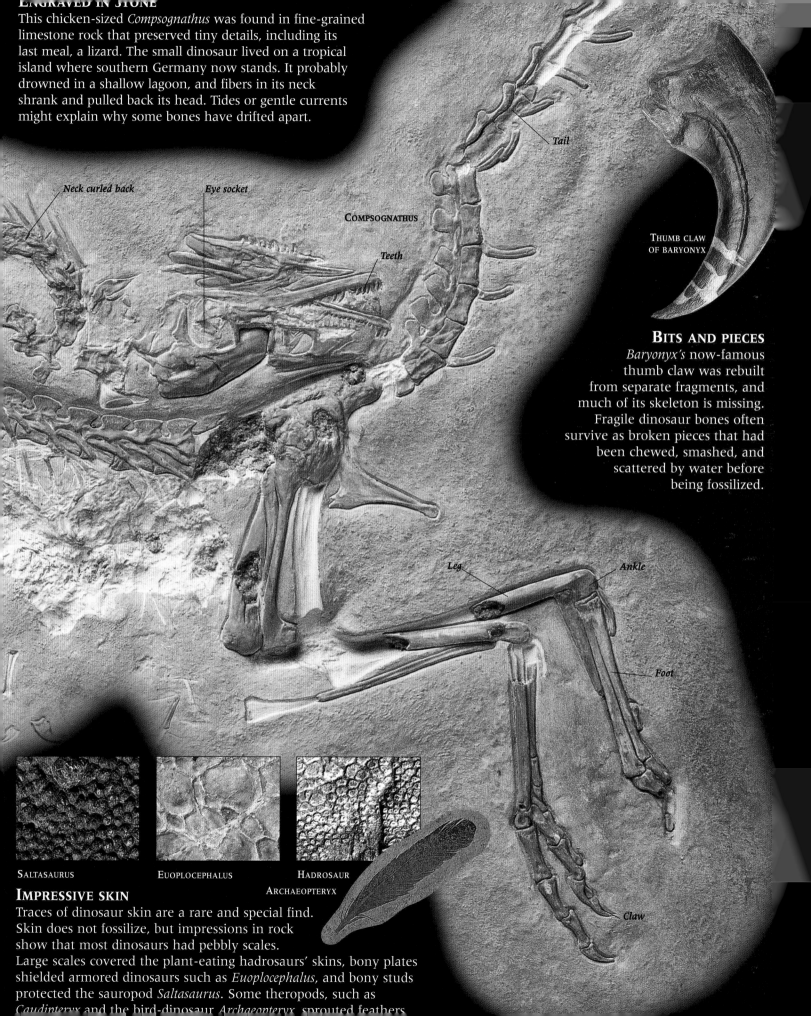

ENGRAVED IN STONE

This chicken-sized *Compsognathus* was found in fine-grained limestone rock that preserved tiny details, including its last meal, a lizard. The small dinosaur lived on a tropical island where southern Germany now stands. It probably drowned in a shallow lagoon, and fibers in its neck shrank and pulled back its head. Tides or gentle currents might explain why some bones have drifted apart.

Neck curled back

Eye socket

COMPSOGNATHUS

Teeth

Tail

THUMB CLAW
OF BARYONYX

BITS AND PIECES

Baryonyx's now-famous thumb claw was rebuilt from separate fragments, and much of its skeleton is missing. Fragile dinosaur bones often survive as broken pieces that had been chewed, smashed, and scattered by water before being fossilized.

Leg

Ankle

Foot

Claw

SALTASAURUS

EUOPLOCEPHALUS

HADROSAUR

ARCHAEOPTERYX

IMPRESSIVE SKIN

Traces of dinosaur skin are a rare and special find. Skin does not fossilize, but impressions in rock show that most dinosaurs had pebbly scales. Large scales covered the plant-eating hadrosaurs' skins, bony plates shielded armored dinosaurs such as *Euoplocephalus,* and bony studs protected the sauropod *Saltasaurus*. Some theropods, such as *Caudipteryx* and the bird-dinosaur *Archaeopteryx,* sprouted feathers.

DINODETECTIVES

JUST AS THE POLICE HUNT for clues at the scene of a crime to solve a mystery, so paleontologists hunt for clues in rocks millions of years old to reveal secrets about the dinosaurs and how they lived. Fossilized teeth, footprints, droppings, and bones can all lead to surprising discoveries; but the most exciting finds are complete skeletons. Excavating a whole dinosaur skeleton can take weeks. Back in the laboratory, teams of scientists analyze every nook and cranny in the bones for clues. Experts on bone damage can tell whether the dinosaur led a violent life or suffered from disease. And plant experts look for traces of leaves and pollen in the rock, which may reveal what kind of environment the dinosaur lived in.

BONE GOLDMINE

These paleontologists are examining the skeleton of a baby *Stegosaurus* embedded in a rock face at Dinosaur National Monument in Utah. Between 1909 and 1924, scientists removed 350 tonnes of dinosaur bones from this quarry. No other site on Earth has yielded so many kinds of late-Jurassic dinosaur. About 1,500 bones remain stuck in the rock for visitors to see.

STEGOSAURUS

Paleontologists take utmost care not to step on their fragile finds or touch them unnecessarily.

CLEANING THE BONES

A paleontologist brushes dirt from a fragile sauropod bone and paints it with hardening liquid. This will help to stop it breaking when it is lifted from the ground. Here in the Sahara, many fossil bones just lie in sand; elsewhere, fossils often have to be pried from hard rock.

PLASTER CAST

In the photograph above, a trench has been dug around the bone and below it. The paleontologists have begun wrapping the bone in bandages and runny plaster. This soon sets hard, protecting the exposed surface of the bone just as plaster casts protect broken legs. The fossil can now be moved

The team lift the precious bone slowly and carefully. If they drop it, it could smash.

HEAVE HO

The excavation team has overturned the bone and finished plastering its underside. Soon a thick plaster jacket completely covers and conceals it. A team of people are needed to lift the heavy object into a truck. Its jacket will safeguard the bone on its long, jolting ride to a museum laboratory for further study

Tail bones of
Stegosaurus

BABY STEGO RIBS

Paleontologists use everyday tools to dig for fossils. Hammers and chisels are used to smash through rock, and trowels to scrape mud. Paintbrushes are useful for removing dust. The smallest tools – including picks and toothbrushes – are used to scratch or brush away the tiniest flecks of rock and dust.

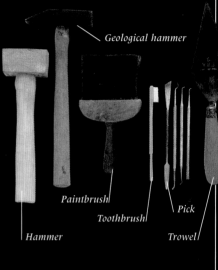

Geological hammer

Paintbrush

Toothbrush

Pick

Hammer

Trowel

BACK IN THE LAB

Inside a museum laboratory, a technician uses a special drill to clean each fossil bone brought in from a dig. First, power saws cut away the outer wrappings of bandages and plaster. Then tiny electric drills and chisels clean off any plaster, soil, or rock still sticking to the fossil's surface. At some museums, fossil skeletons arrive almost completely encased in rock and a sculptor might do the job of chiseling away the rock to reveal the dinosaur hidden inside.

DINO DUNG

This fossilized dinosaur dropping (below) is nearly as long as a man's arm and weighs as much as a 6-month-old child. It probably came from a *Tyrannosaurus*. Inside it are clues about the predator's last meal, such as chewed bits of bone from a plant-eating dinosaur as big as a cow. Studying fossil droppings is one of several ingenious ways in which paleontologists can help to shed light on the lives of the dinosaurs.

Fossilized droppings are called coprolites.

RECONSTRUCTING THE PAST

RECONSTRUCTING A BIG DINOSAUR skeleton from bones found jumbled up in the ground takes years of work by people with specialized skills. First, the bones must be combed from the rock, using all kinds of tools from rock-eating acid to dental drills. Next, paleontologists and model-makers visualize how the animal stood. Technicians construct a lightweight replica of the skeleton, and then engineers erect the replica in a lifelike pose. Ideas about how the dinosaurs stood and moved have changed drastically in recent times. Out are old notions that the dinosaurs lumbered slowly around, dragging their tails. In modern exhibits, they stride on erect limbs, tails held aloft. In a museum in New York City, one *Barosaurus* now even famously rears up on its hind legs.

1. DINOSAUR JIGSAW
Barosaurus's fossil bones spent 60 years in storage at the American Museum of Natural History in New York before a replica skeleton was made. Like a giant jigsaw puzzle, each bone was labeled to show where it belonged in the skeleton.

2. MAKING THE MOLDS
To begin making the replica skeleton, technicians first painted each of the fossil bones with liquid rubber. When the rubber dried, it was peeled off to form a flexible mold. The outside of the mold was strengthened with layers of cotton gauze and a plastic jacket to make the mold stiff.

3. COMPLETING THE MOLDS
Each limb bone was molded in two halves. The inside of each half was painted with liquid plastic – this was to form the outer surface of the replica bones. The plastic was reinforced with fiberglass, and the two halves of each mold were stuck together.

4. FILLING THE MOLDS
Liquid plastic was poured into the hollow molds. This set into a lightweight but rigid foam filled with air spaces. The outer molds were then removed and the foam plastic replica bones painted to match the fossil bones.

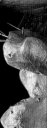

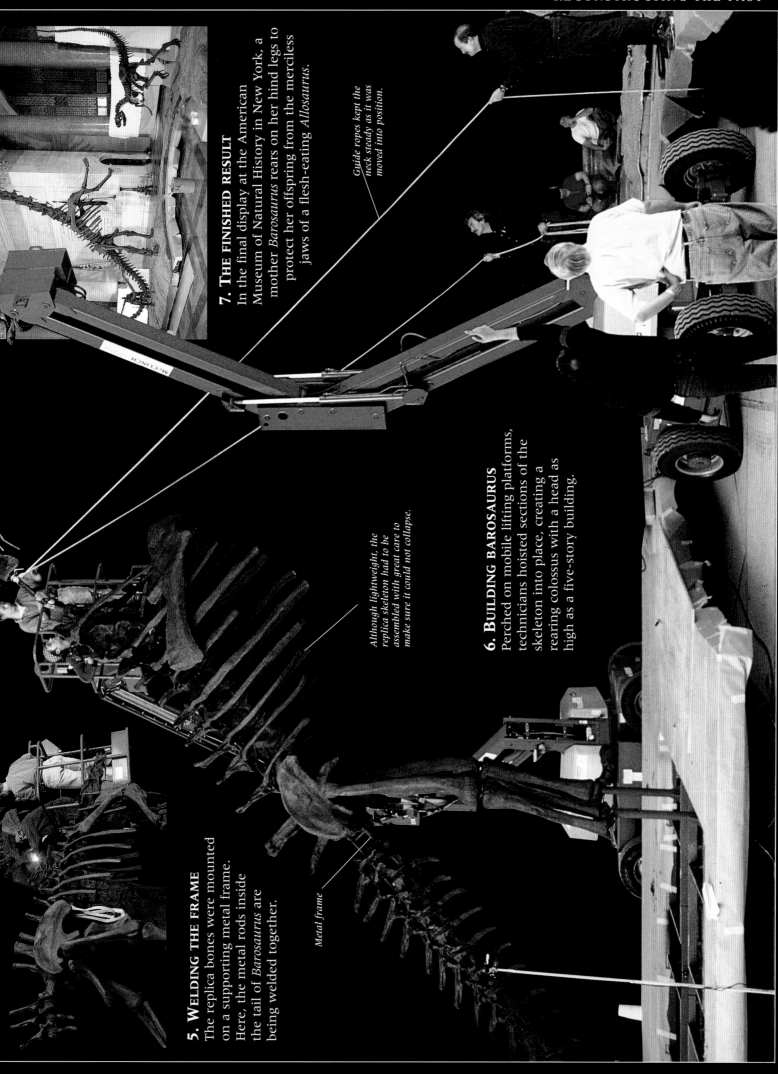

5. WELDING THE FRAME
The replica bones were mounted on a supporting metal frame. Here, the metal rods inside the tail of *Barosaurus* are being welded together.

Metal frame

Although lightweight, the replica skeleton had to be assembled with great care to make sure it could not collapse.

6. BUILDING BAROSAURUS
Perched on mobile lifting platforms, technicians hoisted sections of the skeleton into place, creating a rearing colossus with a head as high as a five-story building.

7. THE FINISHED RESULT
In the final display at the American Museum of Natural History in New York, a mother *Barosaurus* rears on her hind legs to protect her offspring from the merciless jaws of a flesh-eating *Allosaurus*.

Guide ropes kept the neck steady as it was moved into position.

DINODATA

NAMES	PRONUNCIATION	MEANING
Allosaurus	allo SORE uss	strange lizard
Anchisaurus	anky SORE uss	near lizard
Apatosaurus	a PAT oh SORE uss	deceptive lizard
Archaeopteryx	AR kee OP terricks	ancient wing
Argentinosaurus	AR jen TEEN oh SORE us	lizard of Argentina
Barosaurus	barrow SORE uss	heavy lizard
Baryonyx	barry ON icks	heavy claw
Brachiosaurus	brackee oh SORE uss	arm lizard
Brontosaurus	BRON toe SORE uss	thunder lizard
Carcharodontosaurus	kar KAR oh DON toe SORE uss	shark-tooth lizard
Caudipteryx	kor DIP terricks	tail feather
Coelophysis	SEE low FYE siss	hollow form
Compsognathus	KOMP sog NAY thuss	pretty jaw
Corythosaurus	ko RITH oh SORE uss	helmet lizard
Criorhynchus	KRY oh RIN kuss	ram snout
Cryptoclidus	KRIP toe KLIDE uss	hidden closed-tooth
Deinocheirus	DIE no KIRE uss	terrible hand
Deinonychus	die NON ee kuss	terrible claw
Dilophosaurus	die LOAF oh SORE uss	double-crested lizard
Dimorphodon	die MORF oh don	two-form tooth
Diplodocus	di PLOD o kuss	double beam
Dromaeosaurus	DROH mee oh SORE uss	swift lizard
Edmontonia	ED mon TOE nee a	from Edmonton (Canada)
Edmontosaurus	ed MON toe SORE uss	lizard of Edmonton (Canada)
Elasmosaurus	ee LAZ moe SORE uss	plate lizard
Euoplocephalus	YOU owe ploh SEFF a luss	well-shielded head
Gallimimus	gally MEEM uss	chicken mimic
Gastonia	gass TOE nee a	named after Robert Gaston
Giganotosaurus	jig anno toe SORE uss	giant southern lizard
Herrerasaurus	he RAIR a SORE uss	Herrera's lizard
Hypacrosaurus	hye PACK roe SORE uss	nearly highest lizard
Hypsilophodon	HIP sill OFF o don	high-ridged tooth
Ichthyosaurus	ICK thee oh SORE us	fish lizard
Iguanodon	ig WAHN o don	iguana tooth
Lesothosaurus	le SUE too SORE us	lizard of Lesotho
Maiasaura	MY a SORE a	good mother lizard
Mamenchisaurus	ma MEN chee SORE uss	lizard of Mamenchi (China)
Megalosaurus	megga low SORE uss	great lizard
Micropachycephalosaurus	MY krow PAK ee SEFF allo SORE uss	small thick-headed lizard
Minmi	MIN mee	from Minmi (Australia)
Orodromeus	oro DROME ee uss	mountain runner
Oviraptor	oh vee RAP tor	egg robber
Pachycephalosaurus	PACK ee SEFF allo SORE uss	thick-headed lizard
Pachyrhinosaurus	PACK ee RYE no SORE uss	thick-nosed lizard
Parasaurolophus	PA ra SORE oh LOAF uss	like *Saurolophus* (crested lizard)
Pentaceratops	PEN ta SERRA tops	five-horned face
Plesiosaur	PLEASE ee oh sore	ribbon lizard
Protoceratops	PRO toe SERRA tops	first horned face
Pteranodon	ter AN oh don	wing toothless
Pterodactylus	terro DACK till uss	wing finger
Quetzalcoatlus	KWET zal KOH at luss	Quetzalcoatl (Aztec God)
Seismosaurus	SIZE moe SORE uss	earthquake lizard
Spinosaurus	SPY no SORE uss	spine lizard
Stegoceras	steg OSS erass	roofed horn
Stegosaurus	steg oh SORE uss	plated lizard
Styracosaurus	sty RACK oh SORE uss	spiked lizard
Suchomimus	SUE koh MIME uss	crocodile mimic
Torosaurus	torrow SORE uss	bull lizard
Triceratops	try SERRA tops	three-horned face
Troodon	TROH o don	piercing tooth
Tyrannosaurus	tie RAN o SORE uss	tyrant lizard
Ultrasaurus	ultra SORE uss	ultra lizard
Velociraptor	vell OSS ee RAP tor	swift robber

DINOSAUR RECORDS

Biggest dinosaur	*Seismosaurus* 164 ft (50 m) long, 50–150 tons or *Argentinosaurus* length and weight unknown
Biggest predator	*Giganotosaurus* 41 ft (12.5 m) long, 8 tons
Runners up	*Tyrannosaurus* 39 ft (12 m) long, 6 tons *Carcharodontosaurus* 36 ft (11 m) long, 7 tons
Longest predator	*Spinosaurus* 56 ft (17 m) long
Longest neck	*Mamenchisaurus* – 49 ft (15 m)
Largest head	*Pentaceratops* or *Torosaurus* up to 10 ft (3 m) long
Smallest dinosaur	Bee hummingbird of Cuba 0.07 oz (1.95 g)
Shortest non-bird	*Micropachycephalosaurus* 1.6 ft (50 cm) long
Earliest dinosaur	*Herrerasaurus* About 228 million years ago
Most intelligent	? *Troodon* (largest brain relative to body size)
Least intelligent	? *Apatosaurus* (smallest brain relative to body size)
Fastest runner	? *Gallimimus* – 50 mph (80 kmh)
Longest name	*Micropachycephalosaurus*
Shortest name	*Minmi*
Most popular	*Tyrannosaurus*
First in space	*Coelophysis* – fossil taken on board space shuttle in 1998

DIMORPHODON

Dimorphodon
*was not a dinosaur
but a pterosaur,
a reptile that flew.*

TIMELINE

This timeline shows when the main types of dinosaur appeared during the Triassic, Jurassic, and Cretaceous periods. Because they were separated by vast expanses of time and often lived on different continents, most of these dinosaurs would never have met each other.

STEGOSAURUS

DILOPHOSAURUS

HERRERASAURUS

LESOTHOSAURUS

ANCHISAURUS

248 Million years ago (mya)   TRIASSIC   **205 mya**   JURASSIC

GLOSSARY

Ammonite a prehistoric sea creature with a coiled shell.
Ankylosaur a type of dinosaur that had protective armor.
Aquatic to do with water. Aquatic animals live in water.
Binocular vision having two eyes that face forward, so producing a 3D image.
Browser an animal that feeds on bushes and trees.
Camouflage a color or pattern that hides an animal by helping it blend with its surroundings.
Carnivore a flesh-eater.
Carrion dead or rotting animals.
Ceratopsian a type of dinosaur with horns on its face.
Cloaca an opening for feces, urine, sperm, or eggs.
Cold-blooded having a body temperature that varies with the surroundings.
Conifer an evergreen tree that produces seeds in cones.
Continental drift the slow movement of continents across the face of the Earth.
Coprolite a fossilized dropping.
Courtship behavior that forms a bond between a male and female animal before they mate.
Cretaceous the third and last period in the Age of Dinosaurs.
Crocodilian a type of reptile that includes living and extinct crocodiles and alligators.
Cycad a palmlike type of plant that flourished in the Age of Dinosaurs and still survives today.
Digestion the breaking down of food into chemicals that the body can absorb.
Era a great span of time in Earth's history.
Evolution the gradual change that occurs in species over long periods of time.
Extinction the complete dying out of a species.
Fern a type of nonflowering plant with leafy fronds.
Flowering plant a type of plant that reproduces by flowers.
Fossil the remains or trace of a living thing preserved in rock.
Geologist a scientist who studies rocks.
Grazer an animal that eats low-growing plants.
Hadrosaur a type of dinosaur with a beak shaped like a duck's.

Also called a duck-billed dinosaur.
Herbivore an animal that feeds only on plants.
Horsetail a type of non-flowering plant common in the Age of Dinosaurs.
Ichthyosaur a prehistoric sea reptile that looked like a dolphin.
Incubate to keep eggs warm so that they hatch.
Jurassic The second period in the Age of Dinosaurs.
Lizard a type of reptile related to snakes. Dinosaurs are not lizards.
Mammal a type of animal that has hair and feeds its young on milk.
Mammoth a type of prehistoric elephant.
Mesozoic the Age of Dinosaurs.
Migration a long journey to find food or escape bad weather.
Nocturnal active at night.
Omnivore an animal that eats both plant and animal food.
Paleontologist a scientist who studies fossils.
Pangaea a prehistoric continent that contained all the world's land.
Predator an animal that kills and eats other animals.
Prey the victim of a predator.
Pterosaur a type of prehistoric flying reptile with wings of skin.
Reptile a type of vertebrate with lungs and scaly skin.
Sauropod a huge, long-necked type of dinosaur.
Scavenger an animal that eats carrion.
Species a group of living things that can breed together.
Territory an area claimed by an animal.
Theropod a flesh-eating dinosaur.
Tree fern a fern with a trunk.
Triassic the first period in the Age of Dinosaurs.
Vertebrate an animal with a backbone.
Warm-blooded having a body that stays constantly warm. Birds and mammals are warm-blooded.

PROTOCERATOPS

DINOSAURS ON THE WEB

www.bbc.co.uk/dinosaur
Amazing video clips of dinosaurs brought to life by computer wizardry

www.dkonline.com/dino2/private/detect/index.html
Dinodetectives – what goes on behind the scenes on dinosaur digs

www.amnh.org
American Museum of Natural History

dinosaurs.eb.com
Discovering Dinosaurs – an interactive website produced by *Encyclopaedia Britannica*

www.online.discovery.com/exp/fossilzone/fossilzone.html
Hear dinosaur sounds on the Discovery Channel's Fossil Zone website

rexfiles.newscientist.com/nsplus/insight/rexfiles/rexfiles.html
The latest news on dinosaur controversies on *New Scientist*'s "The Rex Files"

www.tyrrellmuseum.com/tour/dinohall.html
Tour the Dinosaur Hall at the Royal Tyrrell Museum, Alberta, Canada

www.ucmp.berkeley.edu/diapsids/dinolinks.html
Dinosaurs in Cyberspace – links to lots of dinosaur websites

www.nhm.ac.uk/museum/galleries
The British Natural History Museum's dinosaur website

www.amnh.org/science/expeditions/gobi/index.html
Dispatches from the Gobi – reports from the American Museum of Natural History's 1998 expedition to the Gobi Desert

www.ndirect.co.uk/~luisrey
Mind-blowing illustrations of dinobirds

ARCHAEOPTERYX

BAROSAURUS

CORYTHOSAURUS

BARYONYX

TRICERATOPS

EUOPLOCEPHALUS

IGUANODON

DEINONYCHUS

TYPES OF DINOSAUR

DINOSAURS CAME IN ALL KINDS of shapes and sizes. Stick-legged midgets crossed paths with lumbering titans that would have dwarfed elephants. Savage carnivores, bristling with claws and fangs, preyed on gentle plant-eaters with toothless beaks and hoofed fingertips. Most dinosaurs were covered in pebbly scales, but some had bony armor-plating set in their skin, and others had an insulating coat of down or feathers, even feathered wings. Thousands of types of dinosaur probably trod the Earth at one time or another. Scientists classify them all according to a family tree that shows how they evolved from the very first dinosaur.

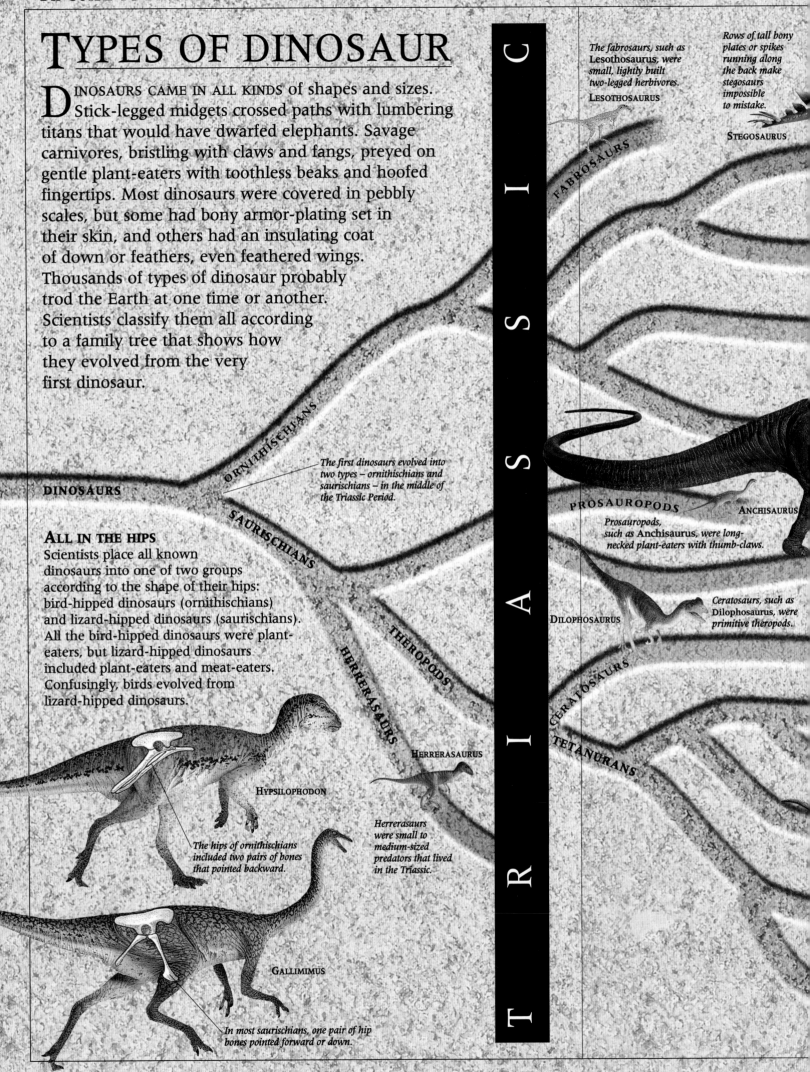

The fabrosaurs, such as Lesothosaurus, were small, lightly built two-legged herbivores.

LESOTHOSAURUS

Rows of tall bony plates or spikes running along the back make stegosaurs impossible to mistake.

STEGOSAURUS

FABROSAURS

ORNITHISCHIANS

The first dinosaurs evolved into two types – ornithischians and saurischians – in the middle of the Triassic Period.

DINOSAURS

SAURISCHIANS

PROSAUROPODS

ANCHISAURUS

Prosauropods, such as Anchisaurus, were long-necked plant-eaters with thumb-claws.

ALL IN THE HIPS
Scientists place all known dinosaurs into one of two groups according to the shape of their hips: bird-hipped dinosaurs (ornithischians) and lizard-hipped dinosaurs (saurischians). All the bird-hipped dinosaurs were plant-eaters, but lizard-hipped dinosaurs included plant-eaters and meat-eaters. Confusingly, birds evolved from lizard-hipped dinosaurs.

THEROPODS

HERRERASAURS

DILOPHOSAURUS

Ceratosaurs, such as Dilophosaurus, were primitive theropods.

CERATOSAURS

TETANURANS

HERRERASAURUS

HYPSILOPHODON

The hips of ornithischians included two pairs of bones that pointed backward.

Herrerasaurs were small to medium-sized predators that lived in the Triassic.

GALLIMIMUS

In most saurischians, one pair of hip bones pointed forward or down.

TRIASSIC

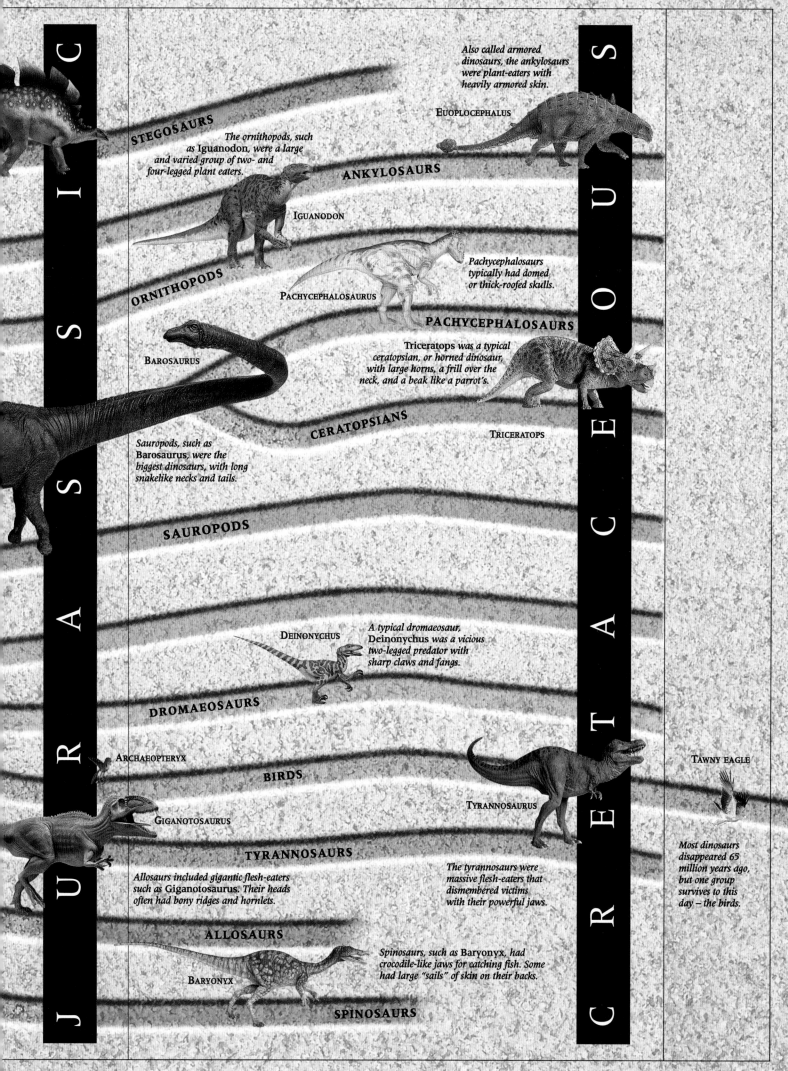

JURASSIC

CRETACEOUS

Also called armored dinosaurs, the ankylosaurs were plant-eaters with heavily armored skin.

EUOPLOCEPHALUS

STEGOSAURS

The ornithopods, such as Iguanodon, were a large and varied group of two- and four-legged plant eaters.

ANKYLOSAURS

IGUANODON

Pachycephalosaurs typically had domed or thick-roofed skulls.

ORNITHOPODS

PACHYCEPHALOSAURUS

PACHYCEPHALOSAURS

Triceratops was a typical ceratopsian, or horned dinosaur, with large horns, a frill over the neck, and a beak like a parrot's.

BAROSAURUS

CERATOPSIANS

TRICERATOPS

Sauropods, such as Barosaurus, were the biggest dinosaurs, with long snakelike necks and tails.

SAUROPODS

DEINONYCHUS

A typical dromaeosaur, Deinonychus was a vicious two-legged predator with sharp claws and fangs.

DROMAEOSAURS

ARCHAEOPTERYX

BIRDS

TYRANNOSAURUS

TAWNY EAGLE

GIGANOTOSAURUS

TYRANNOSAURS

Most dinosaurs disappeared 65 million years ago, but one group survives to this day – the birds.

Allosaurs included gigantic flesh-eaters such as Giganotosaurus. Their heads often had bony ridges and hornlets.

The tyrannosaurs were massive flesh-eaters that dismembered victims with their powerful jaws.

ALLOSAURS

BARYONYX

Spinosaurs, such as Baryonyx, had crocodile-like jaws for catching fish. Some had large "sails" of skin on their backs.

SPINOSAURS

INDEX

ACKNOWLEDGMENTS

Dorling Kindersley would like to thank the following people for their help with this book: Amanda Rayner and Sue Leonard for editorial assistance; Ella Butler for Photoshop work; Luis Rey and Charlie McGrady for the feathered *Velociraptor* model; Sue Malyan for proofreading; Chris Bernstein for the index; Arril Johnson for invaluable advice and a tour of Bristol City Museum. Special thanks also to the producers of dinosaur

websites that feature the latest news.

Dorling Kindersley would also like to thank the following for their kind permission to reproduce their photographs.

(a=above; b=below; c=center; l=left; r=right; t=top)

American Museum of Natural History: 48cl, 49cr; **BBC Natural History Unit:** 53tr; **Bruce Coleman Ltd:** 44–45; Dr Hermann Brehm 26–27; Eric Crichton 30–31; Geoff Dore 22–23; Gerald S. Cubitt 14–15; Jen and Des Bartlett 10bl, 32–33; Jules Cowan 52–53; **DK Picture Library:** 58–59; Centaur Studios 24cr, 25c, 29br; Luis Rey & Charlie McGrady 53cr; Natural History Museum 19cr, 28tc, 29c, 32–33t, 49tr, 54tr, 54–55, 63ca; Naturemuseum Senekenberg, Frankfurt 56cr; Roby Braun 47cr, 54cla, 60bl, 60–61b; Roby Braun 60bc; Stadmuseum Nordlingen 46–47; Royal Tyrrell Museum 12–13,

29cl, 38–39c, 38–39t, 46cl; **Mary Evans Picture Library:** 4tc; **Geoscience Features:** 56–57; **Image Bank:** 24–25; **Kobal Collection:** 50cl; **Nakasato Dinosaur Center:** 26bl; **The Natural History Museum, London:** 13cl, 19tr, 35cl, 50–51, 52cb, 56cl, 56clb, 56bc; Humbolt Museum, Berlin 52bl; John Sibbick 6–7b, 6–7c, 6–7t; **NHPA:** 44cl; GI Bernard 62–63; John Shaw 42–43; **Oxford Scientific Films:** 21br; Matthias Breiter 24–25; Robert A. Tyrrell 9tr; **Peabody Museum of Natural History, Yale University:**

28b; **Planet Earth Pictures:** Gary Bell 34–35; John Eastcott/Yva Momatiuk 36–37; Keith Scholey 4bl; Lythgoe 40–41; M & C Denis-Huot 20–21; Pete Atkinson 18–19; Peter Scoones 33tc; Richard Coomber 10–11; **Reader's Digest:** 48ca; **Science Photo Library:** 51br; D. Van Ravenswaay 50–51; Martin Dohrn/Stephen Winkworth 5tr; Philippe Plailly/Eureilos 57br; Tom Van Sant 6l; **Tony Stone Images:** 8–9; Darryl Torckler 16–17; **Topham Picturepoint:** 8l; **USGS Western Region Geologic Survey:** 57bl.